A Sense of
Measure

SIGNATURE SERIES

A Sense of Measure

by

Robert Creeley

Calder and Boyars

First published as A Sense Of Measure
in Great Britain 1972 by
Calder and Boyars Ltd
18 Brewer Street London W1R 4AS

© Robert Creeley 1973

The following essays were first published in book
form in A Quick Graph: Collected Notes and Essays
in the U.S.A. 1970 by
Four Seasons Foundation
San Francisco, California:

Notes for a New Prose, A Note on the Objective,
To Define, A Dilemma, A Quick Graph, Why
Bother?, Introduction to 'The New Writing in the
U.S.A.', Notes Apropos 'Free Verse', 'I'm Given
to Write Poems'

© Robert Creeley 1970

ISBN 0 7145 0911 6 Cloth Edition
ISBN 0 7145 0912 4 Paper Edition

Printed in Great Britain by
Biddles Ltd, Guildford, Surrey

Grateful acknowledgement is made to the following publications in which these essays and interviews first appeared:

Notes for a New Prose - Origin

A Note on the Objective - Goad

To Define - Artisan

A Dilemma - Black Mountain Review

A Quick Graph - Floating Bear

A Sense of Measure - Times Literary Supplement

Why Bother? - Tish

Notes Apropos 'Free Verse' - Naked Poetry

'I'm Given to Write Poems' - First published in Ein Gedicht und Sein Autor /Lyrik und Essay, Herausgegeben und mit Einleitungen versehen von Walter Höllerer (Berlin, 1967) and subsequently in Harper's Bazaar

The Art of Poetry - Paris Review

The Writer's Situation - New American Review

CONTENTS

NOTES FOR A NEW PROSE

'Language is not reality but another of the
instruments by which man engages reality...'

It is, certainly, reasonable to comment that
Joyce's earlier work presents no such divergence
from normality as does, now, even the mention
of his name. There is, to be got at, a straight
line of impact, search, through the early work,
the poems, the play (which is all 'idea') to the
fact of Ulysses and then, Finnegans Wake. It is
useless to avoid it, or to mistake its point. Which
must be: it is not the content which is changed.
It is the extension of the content into form that has
been tempered, made strong.

To go back. We had been led to believe that
connotation was this: the suggestions of 'meaning'
beyond the supposedly exact, denotative meaning
which custom of usage had put upon the phrase or
word in question. Then, by way of the opening
created by 'associational' content of phrase,
gesture, practice, ways, in short, METHOD -
connotation became meaning versus meaning,
became the fight for sense, in shorthand. (Some
call this 'symbol...') 'It isn't what the words
mean. It's what they mean to you...'

Just so, with Joyce. That is, the possible
suggestions (which can now be called: manifestations) of sense (which was about to become:
value) became the criteria for an ultimate 'sense'

(though no millennium). Because this was done
with language, or, more strictly, within the
words themselves, there we took our sight, a
bead on: what might be up. Wrong from the
start, since it was not words for the sake of
words, but, for the sake of what content, possible,
might shape them, into sense. Taken as such,
Joyce is the craftsman, casting about for a model,
for the model - what is in the head. Not to make
himself, but to make, what is in himself.

Form is the extension of content. This was the
first rule.

2

'A man must create himself, if he is an artist,
instrument also IN ORDER THAT his work be
not expression but illumination...'

Possible arguments for the supposition that
poetry is, now, more able than prose, or more
able to make itself an extension of the present
context, this life, etc., have first to do with the
fact of its ability, (1) to compress, and (2) to
project supposition, as fact. In prose, the lean
toward a 'solution' or a stasis of idea most
usually marks the book as a failure; I mean,
insofar as a writer of prose is willing to give
space to this fixing of idea as the logical 'end' of
movement, etc., just so far we usually won't go
along with him. And I would figure that we are
right. But we deny him, even so, the way out of
it, this fix, or what could get him beyond these
'logics'. Take the idea of a man running along-

10

side a train, taking notes yet. He would be about it, what is now expected - while the poet, at home, can project this iron monster to any place which may please him. It is, then, that we are still confused by the idea of 'reality' in prose. We do not as yet get the basic fact, that reality is just that which is believed, just as long as it is, believed. Poets are more used to this thing: reality as variants round the centre, or, simply, what has been left us.

So how could a prose catch up? Difficult to make the competition actual. It isn't. Elsewhere, it had been pointed out that 'poetry insists upon or suggests a quite different "Universe": a universe of reciprocal relations...' The swing of idea, in stasis - is still poetry. But prose is the projection of ideas, in time. This does not mean that the projection must be an 'actual' one, date by date, etc. The word is law, is the creator, and what it can do, is what any prose can do. There is nothing more real, in essence, about a possible prose than there is about any possible poetry. The ordering of conjecture will remain as 'real' as the ordering of fact, given the right hand.

More to the point, to note the difference, again, between poetry and prose, one of the differences, since there are others as well. Poetry, as the formulation of content, in stasis; prose, as the formulation of content, in a progression, like that of time. This is a simple way of putting it. But sufficient to show that while poetry depends on the flux contained, held within the form, in stasis, prose may intend such a limiting but

cannot justify one. It has no beginning or end.
It has only the length it happens to have. 'Might
be continued...' Just here is the key to its
possible reach, that, in spite of itself, it has to
continue, keep going - cannot stop.

So, in some sense, the usual idea of beginning
and end have put upon prose an order alien to its
nature. This is not to imply a 'necessary chaos'.
It means only that it is, by nature, against
conclusions - or is (as nature is) intent only on
its present. It is the breaking out, of context, of
form, and down or back, always to the progression,
enforced by the nature of its content, and so
determined.

It has neither beginning nor end.

3

'Are we not automatic, to think that because
prose - and - the - novel did, since the 18th, and
conspicuously, in the 19th, and dyingly, in the
20th, do a major job, that it need now be fruitful?'

As soon as the novel, as soon as prose, generally,
supposed for itself, a context other than what it
might, on each occasion make, it had done itself
the greatest possible disservice. And this is not
to be mistaken. We can note, perhaps, that
while poetry may have combined itself in several,
to mean, one thing worked in the hands of several
men, at certain times with success, prose has
never been effectual so taken, as a job, or so
treated. I can remember the notes that Kafka

12

had written about his attempt to write a novel
with Brod - or the more amusing attempts of
Dylan Thomas, etc. Certainly, the novelist
hates his neighbour, hates him for writing, to
begin with, and hates him doubly, for writing
prose. Perhaps this is a false lead. It matters
little except that it can clear the sense of the
necessary singleness of the man who writes
prose. And that any constriction is too much.

The suggestion that record-making can now be
taken as one of the major jobs of those that make
prose is wrong only in its supposition that there
exists any occupation for prose, prior to its
coming. It is wrong in the same way that posit-
ing any 'frame' for prose is wrong. Prose is a
plausible and profitable instrument for making
records. But stories? Novels? One wonders
if it is to the point to set them an end before they
have demonstrated their own. 'As Rousset, e.g.,
wrote L'Univers Concentrationnaire (not Les Jours
de Notre Morte) - and, over a weekend, because
he figured to die the next week of the Causes; or
Martin-Chauffier, who has been a novelist, and
who chose in L'Homme et la Bête to tell not even
what he had heard others say (the last vestige of
the novelist!) but only and precisely what had
happened to him; vide Joe Gould...'

Joe Gould's HISTORY. One wonders. Or, who
put him to such work? Joe Gould.

Pointless to argue such a thing. It is not that
prose cannot be put to such work, that it hasn't
that capability, that it couldn't deal with that end
of things. Rather, like nothing else, it must be

new. And if, say, tradition concerns itself with
these frames, then prose has no tradition. None
whatsoever. It should demand that it has none.
More than we, or they, may have spoken.

It could be, has been, the collection of ideas.
And nothing better, for such documentation. But
records? It was the fact of its perspective, that
made what it gave, of such, reliable. That it is
without, frame. What makes it reliable. That
it owns to no master, that it can't. Its terminals,
ends, are fictitious. Someone dies. 'It was the
end of THAT period...' But continual, that it
repeats, goes over and under, around. Has form,
frame, only as it is such a going. As someone
had said of Stendhal - it all fell into place, exact.

It stands by itself.

4

'The reason why, at this juncture of time, one
fights so hard for prose, is, that it enables him
to get in, to go by, that head of his, to let it play
over his things, outside objects...'

To go back to Joyce. To that mistaking we have
made of him; and you may document this for your-
selves or look to find who has made of those
books something beyond the man who may have
written them. Oddly enough, the most exact
criticism of these things appeared at the same
time that the books themselves did. At least,
that first interest prevented the fatal preoccupations with the 'purpose', of Joyce, with his

own use, as symbol. At least for a time.

Speaking of James, Pound had written that the
logic of the pieces the former had written for
the Yellow Book group was that need to push
beyond the curve, in order to establish it. So,
generally, position is established in prose, and
intention. Hence, this idea of the assumed
obliquity, itself a way of placing something in
the context. Is prose roundabout? It's not that
question which should be asked. Any way could
be the right one. What is got to, what is placed,
would be the better thing to be asking, after it's
done.

Again - de Gourmont's sentence, '...d'écrire
franchement ce qu'ils pensent - seul plaisir d'un
écrivain...' And could it be less, granting it
must be more?

A new prose...Better to think of this, only, as
what may now come. I think we can hang on to
those who have left us something strong enough
to carry over into this time. Prose cannot exist
free of its ability to apply; it can't be faked. So
it would be that Stendhal can still give us the
sense, or one sense, of the order, the 'form',
not to be taken as the form of poetry, nor as we
come back to it, that more basic form of prose.
There is the fact that the more correct translation
of Dostoevsky's Notes from Underground must be
- 'Notes from Under the Floor', or 'Out from the
Cracks like Any Roach.'

Perhaps it will still be necessary to point to the
fact that, while poetry will be the clear, the fact

of the head, prose will be the coming and going.
Around. It is there that it can hit, beyond poetry.
It is not a matter of better or worse. There is
no competition. The drift, in prose, and the way,
of the swing, the reach - we have the necessary
evidence, or I must believe we have.

      I am very old today, the sky is grey,
    I am not very well.
    Nothing can prevent madness.
    As an honourable man who abhors
    exaggeration, I do not know what to do...

We begin, or end, there.

(<u>Origin</u>, No. 2, 1951)

A NOTE ON THE OBJECTIVE

Whether from an altogether 'scientific' attitude,
or from some wish to disassociate, only, by way
of the surface of language, one idea from
another, objectivity has become the apparent
trademark of the careful mind. Common use
would put upon this objectivity the air of the cool
head, that is, one capable of confronting divers
phenomena in their own particulars, rather than
as extensions of one's own senses. It was this
battle, between the objective and the subjective,
then, which had replaced the looser and more
worn fight between classicism and romanticism.

But intentions, as is usual, belie results. Or
are belied by them. Because, however actual an
intention may be, however well considered,
reasoned, etc., its result is not to be found
prior to that act which effects it, and altogether
useless to assume the intended victory before
it's come to pass. In this case, objectivity is,
in intention, the prime aspect of a method which
plans to deal with the 'things around' as
characters in themselves, having as their first
claim on the attention, their own actuality. In
matters of poetry, it amounts to the wish to
transmit, free of imprecise 'feeling', the nature
of 'that' which has moved one to write in the
first place. As such, this wish intends as

complete a break as possible with the subjective.

In effect, this break is not actual, since the writing comes to (1) using this 'that' as a character for use (as content in the poem); and (2) using 'that' as an impetus for the act of writing itself - simply what's pushing. In short, while the first is concerned with abstracting the experience as objective data, the second is equally concerned with keeping it as subjective impulse. And pointless to comment: it's a fight.

A useless fight. However right it may be to damn the use of the subjective method as an excuse for emotional claptrap, it's apt to push us away from any understanding of the subjective in a more basic character, i.e., 'belonging to, or of, or due to, the consciousness...' Impossible to write anything, lacking this relation of its content to oneself. Put another way: things have to come in before they can go out.

Perhaps best to junk both terms, or at least to understand this necessary balance, one with the other. We can't stand outside our content and at the same time we can't eat it like an apple, etc. And perhaps, finally, more to the point than either of these two stances is that one which maintains: a man and his objects must both be presences in this field of force we call a poem.

(Goad, Summer 1951)

18

TO DEFINE

The process of definition is the intent of the poem,
or is to that sense - 'Peace comes of communication.' Poetry stands in no need of any
sympathy, or even goodwill. One acts from
bottom, the root is the purpose quite beyond any
kindness.

A poetry can act on this: 'A poem is energy
transferred from where the poet got it (he will
have some several causations), by way of the
poem itself to, all the way over to, the reader.'
One breaks the line of aesthetics, or that outcrop
of a general division of knowledge. A sense of
the KINETIC impels recognition of force. Force
is, and therefore stays.

The means of a poetry are, perhaps, related to
Pound's sense of the increment of association;
usage coheres value. Tradition is an aspect of
what anyone is now thinking - not what someone
once thought. We make with what we have, and
in this way anything is worth looking at. A
tradition becomes inept when it blocks the
necessary conclusion; it says we have felt nothing,
it implies others have felt more.

A poetry denies its end in any descriptive act, I
mean any act which leaves the attention outside

the poem. Our anger cannot exist usefully without its objects, but a description of them is also
a perpetuation. There is that confusion - one
wants the thing to act on, and yet hates it.
Description does nothing, it includes the object
- it neither hates nor loves.

If one can junk these things, of the content which
relates only to denial, the negative, the impact
of dissolution - act otherwise, on other things.
There is no country. Speech is an assertion of
one man, by one man. 'Therefore each speech
having its own character the poetry it engenders
will be peculiar to that speech also in its own
intrinsic form. '

(Nine American Poets, Artisan, Liverpool: 1953)

A DILEMMA

Why people don't go out and get better jobs, or
finally come to some sense of themselves which
might allow a more profitable exploitation... On
the one hand, there are too many people - you
cannot kill them all, you cannot find a logic quite
sufficient to do this. And if they will not die
quickly enough with sickness, or tiredness, old
age and the like. then at least they can be con-
fined to those places where one will not have to,
simply, consider them.

A logic is fashioned like this, a logic of im-
penetrable worthiness. It follows that, between
a man and his wife, there must be constantly
some means whereby she can spit on him - and
he, likewise, on her. Love, at best, will become
a question of sensation. And on good days she
will sigh, 'my lover...', and on bad days she will
spit, 'my lover...', etc. He will live in a room.
With luck, someone will buy him, i.e., someone
also bought, and so with means, will buy him -
which is the hierarchy of how to live, literally.
To make money - at the first, enough to live on,
by which I mean, to eat with, to be clothed with,
and then, very soon, also to allow that better
stance, to be 'better' clothed, and so on.

But some people, if they are still 'people', have

been removed from this by war, by 'depression' areas, by many things finally, in terms of which they are neither very interesting nor important. And let me make very clear that this is not a question of any bitterness or sentimentality or whatever. Some people cannot 'live' anymore. There is neither reason for them to nor room nor means nor values, nor any of those things by which others, certainly more fortunate, may still claim 'significance'. And by much the same token, it is a little hysterical to feel our own securities are endangered by the specific reality of something like the hydrogen bomb, i.e., suppose one were to instal, say, plumbing in a house, a toilet and all that, and then the toilet is flushed, and, all things being equal - can it be a surprise, or even the point, that (of course!) the toilet flushed?

Heretofore our dangers have been of two kinds, the one (big) metaphoric, and the other (contained) literal. So that to trip on a stone, then, meant, (a) we stubbed a toe (literal) and (b) this pain was token of the possibility of all pain, accident and what might happen (metaphoric). Now enough is accomplished to make an end to that, i.e., we can have the two as one. We can all die at one time.

Which is not, really, a relief. It might be, just as for some people any death not now too painful, not too long, might be. What is there for an alternative except the dreary love too often exercised as it is. Belief - in what. And so on. Dead people already, at best.

I am sorry myself not to care any more, or not to care for much beyond one or two things. That, say, to love anyone becomes more impossible. 'I did love...', one says, etc. I still want to, etc. Perhaps against the distortion, lying, deceit, viciousness, horror, cruelty, and all that, it will still be possible to make that most minimal of defences - at least the knowledge that there might be others likewise confronted.

(Black Mountain Review, Autumn 1954)

A QUICK GRAPH

1. Recent BBC broadcasts of Pound interviews summarize the following:

   (a) Writing: 'You can't have a literature without curiosity. You cannot have a literature without curiosity. And when a writer's curiosity dies out, he is finished. You can do all the tricks you like, but without curiosity you get no literature with any life in it...'

   (b) Literacy: 'A man has a right to have his ideas examined one at a time...' (This parallels another comment made earlier, to the effect: literacy consists of the ability to recognize the same idea in different formulations. Both relate to Pound's insistence on the need to be able to dissociate ideas, i.e., to separate those living from those dead.)

2. Measure - which Dr. Williams continues to hammer at, as in a recent mimeographed sheet, 'The American Idiom':

   'We must go forward uncertainly it may be, but courageously as we may. Be assured that measure in mathematics as

in verse is inescapable, so in reply to
the fixed foot of the ancient line including
the Elizabethans we must have a reply:
it is the variable foot which we are
beginning to discover after Whitman's
advent...'

One academic, Scully Bradley, some
years ago made use of a shifting stress
concept in an attempt to 'scan' Whitman
prompted quite probably by the need to
regularize common to such men; yet he
showed understanding of the fact that the
stress may be variable and yet cohesive
in over-all effect. Too, he made the
point of the rhyming implicit in parallel
or recurrent thought patterns (much as
those used by Allen Ginsberg). Our ears
tell us, certainly, that syllables may be
grouped in a poem in such a way that
they defy usual concepts of metric and
yet maintain a decided rhythm. In
practice this has long been established.
What does need revision is the old
practice of 'phrasal' grouping, qua line,
a loose solution tending to fall apart as
the 'idea' the phrase implies exhausts
itself and/or reaches its end. Poems of
this sort read: The man sat down/ on
the chair / and lifted his foot / into the
air, etc. At no point should the rhythms
peculiar to the given word, in the context
it comes to define, be lost track of. All
rhythm is specific. (Which in turn
explains the boredom implicit in gene-
ralized iambics, etc.)

3. A sense of order - Louis Zukofsky defines one i
   in his essay, 'Poetry':

>'With respect to such action ('utterance',
>i.e., the movement of spoken words
>toward poetry) the specialized concern
>of the poet will be, first, its proper
>conduct - a concern to avoid clutter no
>matter how many details outside and in
>the head are ordered. This does not
>presume that the style will be the man,
>but rather that the order of his syllables
>will define his awareness of order. For
>his second and major aim is not to show
>himself but that order that of itself can
>speak to all men. '

Or reading backwards:

'The choice for science and poetry when
symbols or words stop measuring is to stop
speaking. '

Such order proves as well 'the contest any poet
has with his art: working toward a perception
that is his mind's peace, ' which Zukofsky has
spoken of in <u>Bottom: on Shakespeare</u>.

4. Range - which can be variously characterized:

   (a)   Zukofsky: '...the scientific definition of
         poetry can be based on nothing less than
         the world, the entire humanly known
         world. '

   (b)   Olson's <u>Maximus</u> has built from a like

premise, with the corollary:

> He left him naked
> the man said, and
> nakedness
> is what one means
>
> that all start up
> to the eye and soul
> as though it had never
> happened before

(c)   It is equally Duncan's:

> that foot   informed
> by the weight of all things
> that can be elusive
> no more than a nearness to the mind
> of a single image

Range implies both what there is to deal with, and
the wherewithal we can bring to that activity.
Range describes the world in the limits of
perception. It is the 'field' in the old Pythagorean
sense that 'terms', as John Burnet says, are
boundary stones and the place they so describe
the field itself.

(Floating Bear, No. 2, 1961)

WHY BOTHER?

An art begins prior to its conclusion - which is
why there can be, with great use, an occasion
offering that sense of means which conclusions per
se deny. It can be put more simply. A magazine,
not interested in being either the last word apropos
some function, or taste, or simply a reflection of
what is already 'valued' speciously or not - such
a magazine may define the new possibility by
being, quite literally, the place where it can be
formulated.

No matter what becomes of it, art is local, local
to a place and to a person, or group of persons,
or just what's in the air despite how vague that
sounds. It happens somewhere, not everywhere.
When it does so happen everywhere, it has become
a consequence of taste purely, a vogue or fashion,
and/or what Pound calls 'style of the period' and
definition has given way to a reflection of a given
effect.

No man can work free of the influence of those
whom he may respect in his own art and why
'originality' should imply, in any sense, that he
should, is hard to follow. The light moves, so to
speak, and those who see it have secured an
'originality' quite beyond that qualified by terms
of personality or intent. In poetry, as in other

arts, what is learned is first learned by the
example, that is, by what exists in the art as a
complex definition of possibilities: literally, this
or that poem. Taste operates here as well, of
course, but again Pound is relevant in that he
said, damn your taste, I would like first to
sharpen your perceptions, after which your taste
can take care of itself.

May I submit that when the poem, or the opinion,
or the taste, has come to that security of whatever large magazine - friendly or not - one may
point to, then all has become primarily taste, an
approval of taste, and that the actual work of
definition which allowed taste its turn has gone?

A friend said once of his wife, that she said she
wanted to be a singer, but what she really wanted
to be was famous. One can be famous in many
magazines, but not in those given to the definition
of what a poem, right now, can be. There are
no readers, and there are, even, few writers
who will care to be bothered by what may be an
attention alien to their own. Can you blame a
German, French, English, poet for not caring
specifically about what you face, here and now,
as problems? But can you care for his, if all
your mind is centred on the peculiar structure of
that language given you, to effect, by its forms
and its sounds, what it is, precisely, that you
feel only as a poem? With nothing at all
sentimental about it, and 'Only the poem / only
the made poem, to get said what must / be said...'
as Williams writes all his life.

It is very possible that what one defines, as means

as possibilities, will prove only a temporary instance, a place soon effaced by other use, as when a whole city block is levelled to make a parking lot, or park. But that is the risk. One cannot avoid it, or do otherwise.

I believe in a magazine which is the specific issue of a few men, facing similar problems, places, things. They may, given ability, find the next step all must take if only because they are forced to take each such step with their own feet.

(<u>Tish</u>, September 14, 1962)

A SENSE OF MEASURE

I am wary of any didactic programme for the
arts and yet I cannot ignore the fact that poetry,
in my own terms of experience, obtains to an
unequivocal order. What I deny, then, is any
assumption that that order can be either
acknowledged or gained by intellectual assertion,
or will, or some like intention to shape language
to a purpose which the literal act of writing does
not itself discover. Such senses of pattern as I
would admit are those having to do with a
preparatory ritual, and however vague it may
sound, I mean simply that character of invocation
common to both prayer and children's games.

But it is more relevant here to make understood
that I do not feel the usual sense of subject in
poetry to be of much use. My generation has a
particular qualification to make of this factor
because it came of age at a time when a man's
writing was either admitted or denied in point of
its agreement with the then fashionable concerns
of 'poetic' comment. William Carlos Williams
was, in this way, as much criticized for the
things he said as for the way in which he said them.
I feel that 'subject' is at best a material of the
poem, and that poems finally derive from some
deeper complex of activity.

I am interested, for example, to find that 'automatic or inspirational speech tends everywhere to fall into metrical patterns' as E.R. Dodds notes in his The Greeks and the Irrational. Blake's 'Hear the voice of the Bard' demands realization of a human phenomenon, not recognition of some social type. If we think of the orders of experience commonly now acknowledged, and of the incidence of what we call chance, it must be seen that no merely intellectual programme can find reality, much less admit it, in a world so complexly various as ours has proved.

Recent studies in this country involved with defining the so-called creative personality have defined very little indeed and yet one of their proposals interests me. It is that men and women engaged in the arts have a much higher tolerance for disorder than is the usual case. This means, to me, that poets among others involved in comparable acts have an intuitive apprehension of a coherence which permits them a much greater admission of the real, the phenomenal world, than those otherwise placed can allow. Perhaps this is little more than what Otto Rank said some time ago in Art and Artist concerning the fact that an artist does die with each thing he does, in so far as he depends upon the conclusion of what possibilities do exist for him. Paradoxically, nothing can follow from that which is altogether successful. But again this risk is overcome - in the imagination - by trust of that coherence which no other means can discover. It would seem to me that occasional parallels between the arts and religion may well come from this coincidence of attitude, at least at times when philosophy or psychology are not the measure of either.

Lest I be misunderstood - by 'religion' I mean a
basic visionary experience, not a social order or
commitment, still less a moral one. Gary Snyder
tells me that the Indians consider the experience
of visions a requisite for attaining manhood. So
they felt their enemy, the whites, not men, simply
that so few of the latter had ever gained this
measure of their own phenomenality. In this
sense I am more interested, at present, in what
is given to me to write apart from what I might
intend. I have never explicitly known - before
writing - what it was that I would say. For myself, articulation is the intelligent ability to
recognize the experience of what is so given, in
words. I do not feel that such a sense of writing
is 'mindless' or 'automatic' in a pejorative way.
At the end of Paterson V Williams writes:

-learning with age to sleep my life away:
saying
The measure intervenes, to measure is all we
                                        know...

I am deeply interested in the act of such measure,
and I feel it to involve much more than an
academic sense of metric. There can no longer
be a significant discussion of the metre of a poem
in relation to iambs and like terms because
linguistics has offered a much more detailed and
sensitive register of this part of a poem's activity.
Nor do I feel measure to involve the humanistic
attempt to relate all phenomena to the scale of
human appreciation thereof. And systems of
language - the world of discourse which so

contained Sartre et al. - are also for me a false situation if it is assumed they offer a modality for being, apart from description. I am not at all interested in describing anything.

I want to give witness not to the thought of myself - that specious concept of identity - but, rather, to what I am as simple agency, a thing evidently alive by virtue of such activity. I want, as Charles Olson says, to come into the world. Measure, then, is my testament. What uses me is what I use and in that complex measure is the issue. I cannot cut down trees with my bare hand, which is measure of both tree and hand. In that way I feel that poetry, in the very subtlety of its relation to image and rhythm, offers an intensely various record of such facts. It is equally one of them.

(Times Literary Supplement, August 6, 1964)

INTRODUCTION TO
THE NEW WRITING IN THE USA

Nothing will fit if we assume a place for it. To
attempt to classify writing before one has had
the experience of its activity will be to misplace
it altogether. What can be said is something
itself particular - to senses of form, to the
literal nature of living in a given place, to a
world momently informed by what energies
inhabit it.

1
The forties were a hostile time for the writers
here included. The colleges and universities
were dominant in their insistence upon an idea
of form extrinsic to the given instance. Poems
were equivalent to cars insofar as many could
occur of similar pattern - although each was, of
course, 'singular'. But it was this assumption
of a mould, of a means that could be gained
beyond the literal fact of the writing here and now,
that had authority.

It is the more ironic to think of it, remembering
the incredible pressure of feeling also present in
these years - of all that did want 'to be said', of
so much confusion and pain wanting statement in
its own terms. But again, it is Karl Shapiro's
Essay on Rime (written in the South Pacific at a
military base, 'without access to books, ' in iambic

pentameter) which is successful, and Auden is the measure of competence. In contrast Ezra Pound, H.D., William Carlos Williams (despite the token interest as Paterson begins to be published), Hart Crane and especially Walt Whitman are largely disregarded.

The situation of prose I remember as much the same. Despite the apparent insistence of digression in the work of Joyce, Faulkner, Celine and others who are valued, there is nonetheless the attempt to shape all discussion of their 'form' to the context of an overt pattern, a symbolism, an explanation again anterior to the instance. In short, it is a period when criticism enjoys control of literary reference - so much so, that it can propose itself to be of primary value quite apart from its 'subjects'.

The sense of form which comes of this insistence is defined by Robert Duncan in an essay, Ideas of the Meaning of Form:

> Form, to the mind obsessed by convention, is significant insofar as it shows control. What has nor rime nor reason is a bogie that must be dismissed from the horizons of the mind... Wherever the feeling of control is lost, the feeling of form is lost. The reality of the world and men's habits must be constricted to a realm - a court or a salon or a rationale - excluding whatever is feared... Metaphor must be fumigated or avoided (thought of as displaying the author's fancy or wit) to rid the mind of the poetic where metaphor had led dangerously towards Paracelsus' universe of

psychic correspondences, towards a life where
men and things were beginning to mix and cross
boundaries of knowledge. Poets, who had once
had dreams and epiphanies, now admit only to
devices and ornaments. Love, that had been
a passion, had best be a sentiment or a
sensible affection... The struggle was to have
ideas and not to let ideas have one. Taste,
reason, rationality rule, and rule must be
absolute and enlightened, because beyond lies
the chiaroscuro in which forces co-operate
any sympathies and aversions mingle. The
glamour of this magic haunts all reasonable
men today, surrounding them with, and then
protecting them from, the darkness of possibilities that controls cannot manage, the
world of thought and feeling in which we may
participate but not dominate, where we are
used by things even as we use them.

Confronting such rule, men were driven back
upon the particulars of their own experience, the
literal things of an immediate environment,
wherewith to acknowledge the possibilities of
their own lives. This alternative must now be
familiar, but at that time there were few indeed
to propose it. It is first found for me in
Williams' introduction to The Wedge (1944):

Therefore each speech having its own character
the poetry it engenders will be peculiar to
that speech also in its own intrinsic form...
When a man makes a poem, makes it, mind
you, he takes words as he finds them inter-
related about him and composes them -
without distortion which would mar their exact

significances - into an intense expression of his perceptions and ardours that they may constitute a revelation in the speech that he uses...

It is, in fact, a congruence of 'the darkness of possibilities that control cannot manage' and that 'revelation in the speech' that Williams emphasizes, which informs the first major work of Allen Ginsberg, Howl. He writes of its composition as follows:

By 1955 I wrote poetry adapted from prose seeds, journals, scratchings, arranged by phrasing or breath groups into little short-line patterns according to ideas of measure of American speech I'd picked up from W.C. Williams' imagist preoccupations. I suddenly turned aside in San Francisco, unemployment compensation leisure, to follow my romantic inspiration - Hebraic-Melvillean bardic breath. I thought I wouldn't write a poem, but just write what I wanted to without fear, let my imagination go, open secrecy, and scribble magic lines from my real mind - sum up my life - something I wouldn't be able to show anybody, writ for my own soul's ear and a few other golden ears. So the first line of Howl...

It is relevant that he says, 'I thought I wouldn't write a poem, but just write what I wanted to without fear...' - as does Duncan so emphasize that it was fear that felt 'The reality of the world and men's habits must be constructed to a realm... excluding whatever is feared...' The need becomes, then, literally:

...to recreate the syntax and measure of poor
    human prose and stand before you speechless
    and intelligent and shaking with shame,
    rejected yet confessing out the soul to conform
    to the rhythm of thought in his naked and end-
    less head,
the madman bum and angel beat in Time, unknown,
    yet putting down here what might be left to say
    in time come after death,
and rose reincarnate in the ghostly clothes of
    jazz in the goldhorn shadow of the band and
    blew the suffering of America's naked mind
    for love into an eli eli lamma lamma sabacthani
    saxophone cry that shivered the cities down to
    the last radio
with the absolute heart of the poem of life
    butchered out of their bodies good to eat a
    thousand years.

                              (Howl, Part 1)

2

The usual critical vocabulary will not be of much
use in trying to locate the character of writing
we have now come to. If one depends on the
dichotomy of romantic and classical, he is left
with, too simply, an historical description, itself
a remnant from an earlier 'period'.

The question becomes, what is real - and what is
of that nature? The most severe argument we
can offer against the 'value' of some thing or act,
is that it is not real, that it has no given place in
what our world has either chosen or been forced
to admit. So it is the condition of reality which
becomes our greatest concern - in which relation
the following notes by Charles Olson are most

useful:

> All things did come in again, in the 19th century.
> An idea shook loose, and energy and motion
> became as important a structure of things as
> that they are plural, and, by matter, mass. It
> was even shown that in the infinitely small the
> older concepts of space ceased to be valid at
> all. Quantity - the measurable and numerable
> - was suddenly as shafted in, to any thing, as
> it was also, as had been obvious, the striking
> character of the external world, that all things
> do extend out. Nothing was now inert fact, all
> things were there for feeling, to promote it,
> and be felt; and man, in the midst of it, knowing
> well how he was folded in, as well as how
> suddenly and strikingly he could extend himself,
> spring or, without even moving, go to far, the
> farthest - he was suddenly possessed or re-
> possessed of a character of being, a thing
> among things, which I shall call his physicality.
> It made a re-entry of or to the universe.
> Reality was without interruption, and we are
> still in the business of finding out how all action,
> and thought, have to be refounded...

> ('Equal, That Is, to the Real Itself')

This recognition had come primarily from scientific
thinking, as it might be called - but its evidence
in the way in which the world occurs in Moby Dick
(the object of Olson's discussion) is very striking.
What happens to 'plot' or all such instance of
'category' - the assumption of action as contained,
for example - when all is continuous, 'when the
discrete (isn't) any longer a good enough base for

40

discourse...'? The sentence itself - as Fenollosa
had proposed in The Chinese Written Character
as a Medium for Poetry, and Olson reasserts -
has become 'an exchange of force' in no way a
'completed thought,' since such 'completion' is
impossible in the context of that real which
Melville had apprehended, Olson notes, as 'the
absolute condition of present things...' Let it be
stressed:

> (Melville) put it altogether accurately himself,
> in a single sentence of a letter to Hawthorne,
> written when he was writing Moby Dick (1851):
> 'By visible truth we mean the apprehension of
> the absolute condition of present things.'
>
> (Ibid.)

The context so defined will include such present
statement as this one taken from William
Burroughs' Naked Lunch:

> There is only one thing a writer can write
> about: what is in front of his senses at the
> moment of writing...I am a recording
> instrument...I do not presume to impose
> 'story' 'plot' 'continuity'...

What has been criticized as a loss of coherence in
contemporary American prose - specifically that
of Burroughs and Kerouac - has been, rather,
evidence of this character of the real with which
we are involved. In 'Kerouac's Sound' Warren
Tallman makes a parallel distinction:

> In conventional fiction the narrative continuity

is always clearly discernible. But it is impossible to create an absorbing narrative without at the same time enriching it with images, asides, themes and variations - impulses from within. It is evident that in much recent fiction - Joyce, Kafka, Virginia Woolf and Faulkner are obvious examples - the narrative line has tended to weaken, merge with and be dominated by the sum of variations. Each narrative step in Faulkner's work is likely to provoke many sidewinding pages before a next narrative step is taken. More, a lot of Faulkner's power is to be found in the sidewindings. In brief, what happens in jazz when the melody merges with the improvisations and the improvisations dominate, has been happening in fiction for some time now.

Not only have the earlier senses of 'form' been rejected but equally 'subject' as a conceptual focus or order has given place to the literal activity of the writing itself.

The objects which occur at every given moment of composition (of recognition, we can call it) are, can be, must be treated exactly as they do occur therein and not by any ideas or pre-conceptions from outside the poem, must be handled as a series of objects in field in such a way that a series of tensions (which they also are) are made to hold, and to hold exactly inside the content and the context of the poem which has forced itself, through the poet and them, into being.

(Charles Olson, Projective Verse)

But it is in the nature of the writing itself that
this thinking finds its most active definition - as
here in the final section of John Wieners' 'A
Poem for Painters':

> ...At last. I come to the last defence.
>
> My poems contain no
> wilde beestes, no
> lady of the lake, music
> of the spheres, or organ chants.
>
> Only the score of a man's
> struggle to stay with
> what is his own, what
> lies within him to do.
>
> Without which is nothing
> And I come to this
> knowing the waste,
> leaving the rest up to love
> and its twisted faces,
> my hands claw out at
> only to draw back from the
> blood already running there.

3

Finally, there seems so much that might be said.
The American condition has much to do with
place, an active spatial term which differs in that
way from what has been assumed its European
equivalent. Space, as physical ground, not sky,
I feel to be once again politically active - as it has
always been for the American from the outset. It
is useless, for example, to acknowledge the grow-

ing political weight of either Africa or China without seeing the literal measure these <u>places</u> effect in relation to all senses of the European continuum - in which the American takes its place, at least in part.

But more than that - since 'place' is not now more than activity - there is the question of <u>all</u> terms of relationship, and of the possible con- tinuities of that relationship in a <u>time</u> which is continuous and at all moments 'present' - else it never was.

The point seems that we cannot, as writers - or equally as readers - assume such content in our lives, that all presence is defined as a history of categorical orders. If the nature of the writing is to move in the field of its recognitions, the 'open field' of Olson's <u>Projective Verse</u>, for example, then the nature of the life it <u>is</u> demands a possibility which no assumption can <u>anticipate</u>.

In such a situation the entity of oneself becomes more than a cultural 'programme' and the attempt to recognize its potential has led to experiment with 'consciousness expanding' drugs such as mescaline, and writing which attempts to record such states, as Michael McClure's <u>Peyote Poem.</u>

The impulse is also clear in attempts to rediscover the viable content of terms of life which precede the 'categorical' defined by Aristotle. One does not want to go 'back', merely. But I feel it is true, as Duncan writes, 'We have come so far that all the old stories / whisper once more...' History, as 'progress', seems quite dead.

Otherwise - things as they have taken place so
consistently with us in this country are relevant,
both as condition and as presence. They have
been, always, a basic company, and they involve,
with persistence, our uses of space. Further, I
do not feel that Allen Ginsberg's insistent
equation of states of feeling or being with so-called
'material' things is surreal and/or a dimension
of reality less present in one of its aspects than
in another. There is a persistent literalness in
American writing - very much so in the tradition
with which we are concerned - and it has never
been easily 'symbolic'. 'All the accumulations
of life, that wear us out - clocks, bodies, consciousness, shoe, breasts - begotten sons - your
Communism - "Paranoia" into hospitals...' is
literal reality and literally apprehended. It is -
as Denise Levertov notes from Jung for the title
of one of her poems - that 'everything that acts
is actual, ' and the context may be a street in
broad daylight where reality is just as pervasive
'as a dream' - in fact, is 'the dream' equally with
consciousness.

One cannot describe it, so to speak. Either one
acts in an equal sense - becomes the issue of a
term 'as real as real can be' - or else there is
really nothing to be said. Again, the writing here
collected seems to me distinct in point of its
distance from the usual habit of description - by
which I mean that practice that wants to 'accom-
pany' the real but which assumes itself as
'objectively' outside that context in some way.
Certainly it is possible to minimize or otherwise
distort one's concern in a given matter or relation.
Yet one is either there or not, and being there,

cannot assume some 'not being' so as to 'talk about it'.

I feel, however, that what I am trying to say here comes clearer in Edward Dorn's discussion of Olson's Maximus Poems (with their centre in the town of Gloucester, Massachusetts):

> when the Place is brought forward fully in form conceived entirely by the activation of a man who is under its spell it is a resurrection for us and the investigation is not extractable. And it is then the only real thing. I am certain without ever having been there, I would be bored to sickness walking through Gloucester. Buildings as such are not important. The wash of the sea is not interesting in itself, that is luxuria, a degrading thing, people as they stand, must be created, it doesn't matter at all they have reflexes of their own, they are casual, they do more than you could hope to know, it is useful , it is a part of industry. It has an arrogance of intention. This is the significance of Olson's distrust of Thucydides and his care for Herodotus. It is the significance of Blake's 'the practice of art is antichrist.' Which further means that if you are not capable of the non-functional striking of the World, you are not practising art. Description, letting things lay, was reserved for not necessarily the doubtful, but the slothful, or the merely busy.

4

To tell the story, is all one can do. What

accumulates as the tradition of a craft - its
means, its sophistications - must each time be
reapprehended, not for 'style'. Because as
Louis Zukofsky has taken care to say, of poetry:

> This does not presume that the style will be
> the man, but rather that the order of his
> syllables will define his awareness of order.
> For his...major aim is not to show himself
> but that order that of itself can speak to all
> men.

(<u>Poetry</u>)

That undertaking most useful to writing as an art
is, for me, the attempt to <u>sound</u> in the nature of
the language those particulars of time and place
of which one is a given instance, equally present,
I find it here.

1965

NOTES APROPOS 'FREE VERSE'

I think the term 'free verse' proves awkward just now in that it seems anchored in an opposition to a sense of traditional verse patterns, which are, because of their situation as history, more trusted. 'Free' has such a width of associations - 'free man', 'free fall', 'free prizes', etc. Too, it seems relevant that this sense of verse comes largely from American practice and that its primary figure is Whitman.

It nonetheless provokes a real situation. For example, Yvor Winters' tracking of 'impulse' as informing principle in Emerson's discussions of poetry, as equally in Whitman's, and then in Crane's, cites the significance of this way of stating oneself in poetry as well as the historical range of its occasion. If one thinks of the literal root of the word verse, ' a line, furrow, turning - vertere, to turn...', he will come to a sense of 'free verse' as that instance of writing in poetry which 'turns' upon an occasion intimate with, in fact, the issue of, its own nature rather than to an abstract decision of 'form' taken from a prior instance.

The point is, simply enough, why does the 'line' thus 'turn' and what does inform it in that move-ment? Clearly to say that it is 'free' or equally that it is 'unfree' is to say nothing of much interest. I was impressed a few years ago, reading Joshua Whatmough's Language, to find him saying, as a linguist, that there was no explicit understanding as to why poetry 'turns' in any instance at the precise moment it does - that is, no device of measure then defined could anticipate the precise articulations of this shifting in verse, no matter the verse be 'traditional' or 'free'. Linguistics has, in other respects, qualified usefully the assumptions of traditional metrical systems in making evident the varying 'weights' observable in 'stress' (at least four in number) which had previously been dealt with in patterns which qualified syllables as 'stressed' or 'unstressed' - in short, a very imprecise and clumsy approximation of the activity.

I am myself hopeful that linguistic studies will bring to contemporary criticism a vocabulary and method more sensitive to the basic activity of poetry and less dependent upon assumed senses of literary style. Jacobsen's use of 'contiguity' and 'parallelism' as two primary modes of linguistic coherence interests me. Too, I would like to see a more viable attention paid to syntactical environment, to what I can call crudely 'grammartology.'

However, these are sense of things still far from my own experience in writing. So, briefly, as to that, I feel, as Robert Duncan put it, 'a kind of readiness', much like that makes one feel like taking a walk, some imminence of occasion that has not as yet become literal. I have never, to my own recollection, anticipated the situation of

my own writing in the sense of what I was about
to say. It is certain enough that preoccupations
recur - 'themes', as Duncan has called them -
but how these might gain statement as writing
could not be proposed except as the literal writing
then found means. I was struck by a comment
Franz Kline once made: 'If I paint what I know,
I bore myself. If I paint what you know, I bore
you. So I paint what I don't know...' I write
what I don't know. I feel the situation parallel to
what Pollock suggests by his statement, 'when I
am in my painting...' This, I feel, to be the
condition Charles Olson defines in the key essay,
<u>Projective Verse</u>:

> From the moment (a poet) ventures into
> FIELD COMPOSITION - he puts himself in the
> open - he can go by no track other than the one
> the poem under hand declares, for itself. Thus
> he has to behave, and be, instant by instant,
> aware of some several forces just now be-
> ginning to be examined...

Pound notes Yeats' dependence upon 'a chune in
his head' - and it is that equally, an ordering
that is taking place as one writes, which one
follows much as he might the melodic line of some
song.

The simplest way I have found to make clear my
own sense of writing in this respect is to use the
analogy of driving. The road, as it were, is
creating itself momently in one's attention to it,
there, visibly, in front of the car. There is no
reason it should go on forever, and if one does so
assume it, it very often disappears all too

actually. When Pound says, 'we must understand what is happening', one sense of his meaning I take to be this necessary attention to what is happening in the writing (the road) one is, in the sense suggested, following. In that way there is nothing mindless about the procedure. It is, rather, a respect for the possibilities of such attention that brings Allen Ginsberg to say 'Mind is shapely.' Mind, thus engaged, permits experience of 'order' far more various and intensive than habituated and programmed limits of its subtleties can recognize.

I think each man writing will have some way, so to speak intimate with his own condition. That is, I feel there will be an inherent condition for an ordering intimate to the fact of himself as literal organism. Again, one of the several virtues of Olson's Projective Verse was that of returning to poetry its relation with physiological condition.

For my own part I feel a rhythmic possibility, an inherent periodicity in the weights and durations of words, to occur in the first few words, or first line, or lines, of what it is I am writing. Because I am the man I am, and think in the patterns I do, I tend to posit intuitively a balance of four, a foursquare circumstance, be it walls of a room or legs of a table, that reassures me in the movement otherwise to be dealt with. I have, at times, made reference to my own interest when younger (and continuingly) in the music of Charlie Parker - an intensive variation on 'foursquare' patterns such as 'I've Got Rhythm'. Listening to him play, I found he lengthened the experience of time, or shortened it, gained a very subtle experience of 'weight', all by some decision made within the context of what was called 'improvisation' - but what I should rather call the experience of possibility within the limits of his materials (sounds and durations) and their environment (all that they had as what Pound calls increment of association" but equally all they had as literal condition, their phenomenological fact). There is an interview with Dizzy Gillespie (in the Paris Review, No. 35) in which he speaks of the rhythm particularly in a way I very much respect. If time is measure of change, our sense of it becomes what we can apprehend as significant condition of change - in poetry as well as in music.

In any case Williams showed me early on that rhythm was a very subtle experience, and that words might share equivalent duration even though 'formally' they seemed in no way to do so. Pound said , 'LISTEN to the sound that it makes, ' and Olson, in like emphasis, made it evident that we could only go 'By ear. '

Finally, there was and is the fact of, what it was one had to say - in Louis Zukofsky's sense, 'Out of deep need...' I never spoke easily and had to write, for the most part, just as adamantly. There is a section of Williams' The Desert Music which might be my own:

You seem quite normal. Can you tell me? Why does one want to write a poem?

        Because it's there to be written.

Oh. A matter of inspiration then?

Of necessity.

Oh. But what sets it off?

        I am that he whose brains
        are scattered
        aimlessly...

Why after all say any of this - but for some fear
one is not 'doing it right' and isn't that, even,
the occasion for such argument as still can exist
on the subject of 'free verse', which is at best
some 'historical' label. Williams, at the end of
The Desert Music, says all that anyone can:

                        I am a poet! I
am. I am. I am a poet, I reaffirmed, ashamed

Now the music volleys through as in
a lonely moment I hear it. Now it is all
about me. The dance! The verb detaches itself
seeking to become articulate

        And I could not help thinking
        of the wonders of the brain that
        hears that music and of our
        skill sometimes to record it.

                        December 11, 1966

(Naked Poetry, edited by Stephen Berg
               and Robert Mezey, 1969)

'I'M GIVEN TO WRITE POEMS'

I'm <u>given</u> to write poems. I cannot anticipate
their occasion. I have used all the intelligence
that I can muster to follow the possibilites that
the poem 'underhand', as Olson would say, is
declaring, but I cannot anticipate the necessary
conclusions of the activity, nor can I judge in
any sense, in moments of writing, the significance
of that writing more than to recognize that it is
being <u>permitted</u> to continue. I'm trying to say
that, in writing, at least as I have experienced it,
one is <u>in</u> the activity, and that fact itself is what
I feel <u>so</u> deeply the significance of anything that
we call poetry.

For some sense, then, of how it was I came to be
involved with poetry, at the outset I was much
more interested in <u>writing</u> apart from its desig-
nated modes, and perhaps I am characteristically
American in that respect. To begin with, I was
shy of the word 'poet' and all its associations in
a world I was then intimate with. It was not, in
short, a fit attention for a young man raised in
the New England manner, compact of Puritanically
deprived senses of speech and sensuality. Life
was real and life was earnest, and one had best
get on with it. The insistent preoccupation with
words did begin for me early, just that I did want
so much to know what people were saying, and

what, more precisely, they meant by it.

I think the most significant encounter for me as a young man trying to write was that found in the work of William Carlos Williams. He engaged language at a level both familiar and active to my own senses, and made of his poems an intensively emotional perception, however evident his intelligence. Despite his insistence on his Mediterranean connections, so to speak, he was as Puritan as I - or Lawrence or Thoreau or the Melville of Pierre.

Otherwise, the forties - the time in which I came of age - were complicated in many bitter ways indeed. Not the least of the problems then evident for someone trying to realize him or herself in the world was the confusion about the very nature of 'literature' itself. Coming from New England, I felt awkwardness about books to begin with, because they were for me often instances of social mark or measure, even at times a privilege of intellectual order - just as Hardy speaks of them in Jude the Obscure. I was very shy about communicating my own commitments in reading, and yet I used books as a very real place to be. Not merely an escape from the world - the difficulty was how to get into it, not away - books proved a place very deeply open to me, at moments of reading, in a sense few others were ever to be.

Thinking of that, let me note kinship with another writer - Robert Duncan - who has played a very important role in my life, both as mentor, very often, and as one whom I feel to share with me this particular sense of world, and writing, and poetry, which I most deeply respect. In a collection of his called The Opening of the Field, significantly enough, the first poem begins:

OFTEN I AM PERMITTED TO RETURN TO A MEADOW

Then continues:

> as if it were a scene made-up by the mind,
> that is not mine, but is a made place,
> that is mine, it is so near to the heart,
> an eternal pasture folded in all thought
> so that there is a hall therein
>
> that is a made place, created by light
> wherefrom the shadows that are forms fall.

This sense of a poem - that place, that meadow - has echoes of so many things that are intimate to my own sense of the reality experienced in writing. One would find that field or 'meadow' in Whitman also, and it would be equally the sense of place I feel Allen Ginsberg many times to be entering, to be speaking of or longing for. Charles Olson too possesses its occasion in his sense of 'open' verse or that open field, as he insists upon it, in composition. I have found it deeply in H.D.'s writing: 'I go where I love and am loved...' And in Pound's 'What thou lovest well remains, / the rest is dross...'

> What thou lov'st well shall not be reft from thee
> What thou lov'st well is thy true heritage
> Whose world, or mine or theirs
>   or is it of none?

First came the seen, then thus the palpable
            Elysium, though it were in the halls of hell,
What thou lovest well is thy true heritage...

All of these are, to my own mind, not only tokens
but evidences of a place, a very distinct and
definite place, that poetry not only creates but
itself issues from - and one in writing is, as
Duncan says, 'permitted to return', to go there,
to be in that reality. There is a poem by Allen
Ginsberg which has always moved me deeply. He
calls it simply 'Song' and it is included in the first
collection of his poetry, Howl. The closing lines
of this poem are:

    yes, yes,
            that's what
    I wanted,
            I always wanted,
    I always wanted,
            to return
    to the body
            where I was born

That body is the 'field' and is equally the experience of it. It is, then, to 'return' not to oneself as some egocentric centre, but to experience
oneself as in the world, thus, through this agency
or fact we call, variously, 'poetry'.

In the same passage quoted from Duncan, there is
another sense of much interest to me in the
emphasis he puts upon 'made': 'a scene', as he
says, 'made-up by the mind, /that is not mine,
but is a made place, / that is mine...' And again,
two lines following: 'there is a hall therein/ that

is a made place...' This emphasis takes its occasion from the sense of poet as maker, going back to the Greek root, <u>poiein</u>, 'to make'.

One of the few books I've ever had that was stolen - not by me, as it happened, but by a girl I persuaded to steal it for me - was William Carlos Williams' <u>The Wedge</u>. It proved <u>fire</u> of a very real order, and, for the record, <u>was</u> subsequently stolen from me in turn when I was teaching at Black Mountain in the mid-fifties. In 1944, when it was first published and shortly after which I got hold of it, its content was a revelation to me. In the preface Williams makes this statement:

> When a man makes a poem, makes it, mind you, he takes words as he finds them inter-related about him and composes them - without distortion which would mar their exact significances - into an intense ex-pression of his perceptions and ardours that they may constitute a revelation in the speech that he uses. It isn't what he <u>says</u> that counts as a work of art, it's what he <u>makes</u>, with such intensity of perception that it lives with an intrinsic movement of its own to verify its authenticity.

I think this is very much the way Americans are given to speak - not in some dismay that they haven't another way to speak, but, rather, that they feel that they, perhaps more than any other group of people upon the earth at this moment, have had both to imagine and thereby to <u>make</u> that reality which they are then given to <u>live</u> in. It is as though they had to <u>realize</u> the world anew.

They are, as Charles Olson says, 'the last first people'. Now, in contemporary fact, they are also the oldest issue of that imagination - even in some ways bitterly so, because they have thus inherited the world as not only a place to live in, but also as that reality for which they are responsible in every possible sense.

However, I would mistake my own experience of poetry if I were to propose it as something merely intentional, and what men may imagine, either as worlds or poems, is not simply a purpose either may satisfy. Williams also had no sense of patness in the making of a poem, or of a world - but felt, as he says in one of his own poems:

Be patient that I address you in a poem,
        there is no other
                        fit medium.
The mind
        lives there. It is uncertain,
                        can trick us and leave us
agonized. But for resources
        what can equal it?
                        There is nothing. We
should be lost
        without its wings to
                        fly off upon.
The mind is the cause of our distresses
        but of it we can build anew.
                        Oh something more than
it flies off to:
        a woman's world,
                        of crossed sticks, stopping
thought. A new world
        is only a new mind.

                              And the mind and the poem
            are all apiece.

To put it simply indeed, it is not the intention to
write that matters, but that one can - that such a
possibility can exist in which the mind may make
evident its resources apart from the limits of
intention and purpose.

In The Desert Music - for myself the loveliest
form he left us - Williams makes further qualification of the poem in its peculiar and singular
function of making real:

                              Only the poem
            only the made poem, to get said what must
            be said, not to copy nature, sticks
            in our throats

            The law? The law gives us nothing
            but a corpse, wrapped in a dirty mantle.
            The law is based on murder and confinement,
            long delayed,
            but this, following the insensate music,
            is based on the dance:
                              an agony of self-realization
            bound into a whole
            by that which surrounds us
                                        I cannot escape
            I cannot vomit it up
            Only the poem!

            Only the made poem, the verb calls it
                                        into being.

Act becomes the primary issue of 'verb' or verbum,

a word. 'In the beginning was the Word' - and
the word was the reality of the imagination. The
'music', which the poem's title emphasizes and
which becomes so central a content in the poem's
activity is that which vivifies, the anima mundi,
lifeness and/or life itself. Our response to it
or what it creates, its effects in the reality we
are given, is the 'dance. '

> Now the music volleys through as in
> a lonely moment I hear it. Now it is all
> about me. The dance! The verb detaches itself
> seeking to become articulate

Poems are very specific kinds of dancing, because
language is that possibility most specific to our
condition as human beings. But I do not speak
easily of these things because I feel, always, a
timidity and confusion trying to isolate a sense
that can only be experienced in the literal fact of
the poem itself. It is as though I were trying to
make actual a sense of wetness apart from water
itself.

It is possible, nonetheless, to continue now to use
those men I have used so much, to make evident
what senses of poetry have been for me insistent.
In Maximus, to Gloucester Charles Olson gives
measure of the occasion in a way that informs my
own:

> He left him naked,
> the man said, and
> nakedness
> is what one means
> that all start up

to the eye and soul
as though it had never
happened before

My sense of his statement is this: in the fact of
our lives we are brought to primary situations,
primary terms of experience - what they might
have meant by 'first things first' but probably
didn't. 'Nakedness' is to stand manifestly in
one's own condition, in that necessary freshness,
however exposed, because all things are particular
and reality itself is the specific content of an
instant's possibility. In poems we realize, not
in discursive or secondary manner, but with this
implicit and absolutely consequential fact of
firstness, terms of our own life, manifestations
of that life which, otherwise, are most awkwardly
acknowledged. It is, again, that 'field' that
Robert Duncan speaks of as being 'permitted' to
enter. First things. We arrive in poems at the
condition of life most viable and most primal in
our own lives.

I've said that I feel myself to be a poet who is
given to write. And I'm even awkward about
using that designation, that is, to call myself so,
a poet - because I do not feel I have that decision
in it. Yet the complexity of the dilemna seems to
me a very real one. How shall we understand
Williams' painfully marked insistence just before
the close of The Desert Music:

                    I am a poet! I
     am. I am. I am a poet, I reaffirmed, ashamed

In America, we are certainly not poets simply,

nor much of the time.

The saints of my own calendar are saints of this
exposure, beginning with Columbus and like men
whose imagination realized, reified, one might
say, the world I live in. They are Poe - who,
as Williams makes clear, forced the local to
yield him a world apart from the habits of English
manner; Whitman - for the permission of life he
insisted upon; Melville - the primary imagination
of the isolation of our condition; Pound - who,
like any Yankee, makes intelligence an invention
of necessity; Hart Crane - whose 'failure' regained
the possibility of our response to what we are
given to feel. It may well be that in the absence
of such allusive society as European literature, in
its own condition, has necessarily developed, that
the American in contrast must so realize each
specific thing of his own - 'as though it had never /
happened before.' I think of Williams' sharply
contemptuous answer to the British English
professor, met with in Seattle, Washington, of all
places, who asked him after a reading, 'where he
got his language' - to which Williams replied,
'Out of the mouths of Polish mothers' - meaning
not Polish, but the harsh, crude, blocked 'poor
English' of those immigrant women he had as
patients in his profession as a doctor. My 'saints',
then, are those men who defined for me an
explicit possibility in the speech that I was given
to use, who made the condition of being American
not something chauvinistically national but the
intimate fact of one life in one place at one time.

To speak then of the writing itself, which I can do
only tentatively - just that I am persuaded by

Heisenberg that 'observation impedes function'
- I have again much depended upon senses of
procedure and examples (which are, of course,
the point) given me by such men. In the forties
there was so much talk about the poem, about
levels of meaning, ambiguities, symbols, allusions.
It was even felt that criticism itself would prove
the most significant literary activity of the time.

Pound, in contrast, spoke of the literal condition
of the writing, and it was he I used as guide - and
continue to now, twenty years later, because his
advice proved facts of perception as active to my
mind now as when I first came to them. For
example, his quotation from Rémy de Gourmont,
'Freely to write what one chooses is the sole
pleasure of a writer,' continues for me the only
actual measure of the occasion I am aware of. He
gave me the experience of integrity as 'Man
standing by his word.' More, he spoke so clearly
of the explicit situation of writing:

> In making a line of verse (and thence
> building the lines into passages) you have
> certain primal elements:
> That is to say, you have the various
> 'articulate sounds' of the language, of its
> alphabet, that is, and the various groups of
> letters in syllables.
> These syllables have differing weights
> and durations
> > A. original weights and durations
> > B. weights and durations that seem
> >   naturally imposed on them by
> >   the other syllable groups around
> >   them.

Those are the medium wherewith the poet cuts his design in TIME.

Against the arguments of taste and opinion which criticism so largely depends upon, Pound called attention to the character of the activity:

Rhythm is a form cut into TIME, as a design is determined SPACE...

LISTEN to the sound that it makes...

However it is really Charles Olson I must thank for whatever freedom I have as a poet, and I would value him equally with Pound and Williams and those others I have mentioned. Freedom has always been for me a difficult experience in that, when younger, I felt it had to propose senses of experience and of the world I was necessarily not in possession of - something in that way one might escape to. I mistook, I think, the meaning of 'freely to write what one chooses,' which both de Gourmont and Pound may well have had in mind, because I took 'freely' to mean 'without significant limit' and 'chooses' to be an act of will. I therefore was slow in realizing the nature of Olson's proposal, that 'Limits / are what any of us / are inside of', just that I had taken such 'limits' to be a frustration of possibility rather than the literal possibility they in fact must provoke. Despite Pound - or rather, because I could not hope to gain such means as he had - I had to find my own way and at first I was com-pletely ignorant of what it might be.

In consequence, what Olson made clear to me

during the late forties and early fifties was of
very great use. I am speaking of the kind of
thinking that is evident in his essay, Projective
Verse, written during the same time. Let me
quote an instance:

> The objects which occur at every given
> moment of composition (of recognition, we can
> call it) are, can be, must be treated exactly
> as they do occur therein and not by any ideas
> or preconceptions from outside the poem,
> must be handled as a series of objects in field
> in such a way that a series of tensions (which
> they also are) are made to hold, and to hold
> exactly inside the content and the context of
> the poem which has forced itself, through the
> poet and them, into being.

Not long ago, in conversation, Robert Duncan
qualified his sense of choice as being recognition,
that is, choice is significantly the act of
recognition, and I believe it. What one 'chooses'
in writing is importantly of this nature, for me,
and composition is the fact and effect of such
activity. One isn't putting things into poems, then,
at least not as my own experience of writing informs me. There is never a 'subject' about which
one constructs an activity called 'poetry'. Nor
can one, as Williams says, 'copy nature', take
from that which is elsewise informed some
felicitous appearance, whether a rhyme or a so-
called sentiment.

However best it might be put, what Olson made
evident to me was that writing could be an intensely specific revelation of one's own content,

and of the world the fact of any life must engage.
It has nothing to do with 'personalism' - which,
like personality, is a mirror or reflective image
sense, a cosmetic of intentions. On the contrary,
what emerges in the writing I most value is a
content which cannot be anticipated, which 'tells
you what you don't know', which you subvert,
twist, or misrepresent only on peril of death.

What I have written I knew little of until I had
written it. If at times I have said that I enjoy what
I write, I mean that writing is for me the most
viable and open condition of possibility in the
world. Things have happened there, as they have
happened nowhere else - and I am not speaking of
'make-believe', which, be it said, is 'as real as
real can be'. In poems I have both discovered and
born testament to my life in ways no other possibility has given me. Can I like all that I may
prove to be, or does it matter? Am I merely
living for my own approval? In writing it has
seemed to me that such small senses of existence
were altogether gone, and that, at last, the
world 'came true'. Far from being its limit or
director, the wonder is that I have found myself
to be there also.

(Lecture delivered at the Literarisches
Colloquium, Berlin, January 1967; published
in Ein Gedicht und sein Autor / Lyrik und
Essay, Herausgegeben und mit Einleitungen
versehen von Walter Höllerer (Berlin, 1967),
and in Harper's Bazaar, July 1967)

INTERVIEWER. What do you think was the first impulse that set you on the course to being a writer?

CREELEY. As a kid I used to be fascinated by people who, like they say, 'travelled light'. My father died when I was very young, but there were things of his left in the house which my mother kept as evidences of his life: his bag, for example, his surgical instruments, even his prescription pads. These things were not only relics of his person, but what was interesting to me was that this instrumentation was peculiarly contained in this thing that he could carry in his hand. The doctor's 'bag'. One thinks of the idiom which is so current now 'bag', to be in this or that 'bag'. The doctor's bag was an absolutely explicit instance of something you carry with you and work out of. As a kid, growing up without a father, I was always interested in men who came to the house with specific instrumentation of that sort - carpenters, repairmen - and I was fascinated by the idea that you could travel in the world that way with all that you needed in your hands. a Johnny Appleseed. All of this comes back to me when I find myself talking to people about writing. The scene is always this: 'What a

great thing! To be a writer! Words are something you can carry in your head. You can
really "travel light" '

INTERVIEWER. You speak a great deal about
the poet's locale, his place, in your work. Is
this a geographic term, or are you thinking of
an inner sense of being?

CREELEY. I'm really speaking of my own sense
of place. Where 'the heart finds rest', as
Robert Duncan would say. I mean that place
where one is open, where a sense of defensive-
ness or insecurity and all the other complexes
of response to place can finally be dropped.
Where one feels an intimate association with
the ground under foot. Now that's obviously
an idealization - or at least to hope for such a
place may well be an idealization - but there
are some places where one feels the possibility more intensely than others. I, for
example, feel much more comfortable in a
small town. I've always felt so, I think,
because I grew up in one in New England. I
like that spill of life all around, like the spring
you get in New England with that crazy water,
the trickles of water everywhere, the moisture,
the shyness, and the particularity of things
like bluejays, I like the rhythms of seasons,
and I like the rhythms of a kind of relation to
ground that's evident in, say, farmers; and I
like time's accumulations of persons. I loved
aspects of Spain in that way, and I frankly have
the same sense of where I now am living in
New Mexico. I can look out the window up into
hills seven miles from where the Sandia Cave

is located, perhaps the oldest evidence of man'
occupation of this hemisphere. I think it dates
back to either 15, 000 or 20, 000 B.C. and it's
still there. And again I'm offered a scale,
with mountains to the southeast, the Rio Grande
coming through below us to the west, and then
that wild range of mesa off to the west. This
is a very basic place to live. The dimensions
are of such size and of such curious eternity
that they embarrass any assumption that man
is the totality of all that is significant in life.
The area offers a measure of persons that I
find very relieving and much more securing to
my nature than would be, let's say, the
accumulations of men's intentions and exertions
in New York City. So locale is both a geographic term and the inner sense of being.

INTERVIEWER. Do you credit any one writer -
ancestor or contemporary - with a strong
influence on your poetry?

CREELEY. I think Williams gave me the largest
example. But equally I can't at all ignore
Charles Olson's very insistent influence upon
me both in early times and continuingly. And
Louis Zukofsky's. The first person who
introduced me to writing as a craft, who even
spoke of it as a craft, was Ezra Pound. I
think it was my twentieth birthday that my
brother-in-law took me down to a local book-
store in Cambridge and said, 'What would you
like? Would you like to get some books?' I
bought Make It New and that book was a revelation to me. Pound spoke of writing from the
point of view of what writing itself was, not

what it was 'about'. Not what symbolism or structure had led to, but how a man might address himself to the act of writing. And that was the most moving and deepest understanding I think I have ever gained. So that Pound was very important to my craft, no matter how much I may have subsequently embarrassed him by my own work. So many, many people - Robert Duncan, Allen Ginsberg, Denise Levertov, Paul Blackburn, Ed Dorn. I could equally say Charlie Parker - in his uses of silence, in his rhythmic structure. His music was influential at one point. So that I can't make a hierarchy of persons.

INTERVIEWER. How about communicating with other writers when you were beginning?

CREELEY. I started writing to Ezra Pound and William Carlos Williams about a magazine I was involved in. That's how I got up courage to write them. I would have been too shy just to write them and say, 'I think you are a great man.' To have business with them gave me reason. Pound wrote specifically, but he tended to write injunctions - 'You do this. You do that. Read this. Read that.'

INTERVIEWER. Did you do everything he said?

CREELEY. I tried to. I couldn't do it all. He would send books at times which would be useful. The History of Money by Alexander Del Mar, which I read, and thought about. He was very helpful. It was very flattering to be taken seriously by him. Williams was always much

more specific. At times he would do things
which would... not <u>dismay</u> me, - but my own
ego would be set back. I remember one time
I wrote him a very stern letter - some
description about something I was going to do,
or <u>this</u> was the way things were, <u>blah, blah</u>.
And he returned me the sheets of the letter
and he had marked on the margin of particular
sections 'Fine. Your style is tightening.'
But I had the sense to know such comments
were of more use to me than whether or not
he approved of what I had to say. He would do
things like that which were very good. While
Pound would say, 'Would you please tell me
how old you are? You refer to having been
involved in something for forty years. Are
you twenty-three, or sixty-three?'

INTERVIEWER. At this point were you raising
pigeons in the country?

CREELEY. As a kid I'd had poultry, pigeons and
chickens and what not. I'd married in 1946 and
after a year on Cape Cod, we moved to a farm
in New Hampshire where I attempted so-
called sustenance farming. We had no ambitions
that this would make us any income. We had a
small garden that gave us produce for canning.
It made the form of a day very active and
interesting, something continuing - feed them,
pluck them, take care of them in various
ways. And I met a lovely man, a crazy, decisive breeder of Barred Rocks. He was quite
small, almost elfin in various ways, with this
crazy, intense, and beautifully articulate
imagination. He could <u>douse</u> for example, and

all manner of crazy, mystical business that he took as comfortably as you'd take an axe in hand. No dismay, or confusion at all. A neighbour in New Hampshire would lose money in the woods. So he'd just cut a birch wand, and find it. The same way you'd turn on the lights to see what you're doing. I remember one of these neighbours of ours, Howard Ainsworth, a woodcutter, was cutting pulp in the woods on a snowy day. But he had a hole in his pocket, and by the time he had discovered it, he'd lost a pocketful of change. So Howard simply cut himself a birch stick and he found it. It was nearly total darkness in the woods. He only remarked upon it, that is, how he'd found it, as an explanation of how he'd found it. I mean, it never occurred to him that it was more extraordinary than that.

INTERVIEWER.   How did it occur to you?

CREELEY.   I was fascinated by it - because it was a kind of 'mysticism' which was so extraordinarily practical and unremoved. He had this crazy, yet practical way of exemplifying what he knew as experience. He used to paint, for example. Once he showed me this picture of a dog. He said, 'What do you think of this? It's one of my favourite dogs. ' It was this white and black dog standing there looking incredibly sick. And I said, 'Well, it's a nice picture. But. ' And he said, 'Yes, it died three days later. That's why it looks so sick. ' He delighted me, you know, and I felt much more at home with him than with the more - not sophisticated - because I don't think any

man was more sophisticated in particular
senses than he, but, God, he talked about
things you could actually put your hand on.
He would characterize patience, or how to pay
attention to something.

INTERVIEWER. Do you think you work better in
the isolated places you seem to frequent - in
New Hampshire, Mallorca, New Mexico?

CREELEY. That seems to be my habit, although
having been a teacher for some years I can
make it with a number of people and find a
place with them. But my dilemma, so to
speak, as a younger man, was that I always
came on too strong with people I casually met.
I remember one time, well, several times, I
tended to go for broke with particular people.
As soon as I found access to someone I really
was attracted by - not only sexually, but in the
way they were - I just wanted to, literally, to
be utterly with them. I found myself absorbing
their way of speaking. I just wanted to get in
them. And some people, understandably, would
feel this was pretty damned exhausting - to have
someone hanging on, you know, like coming at
you. I didn't have any experience of how it was
really affecting the other person. I mean I
think that a lot of my first wife's understandable
bitterness about our relationship was the
intensity that she was having to deal with. I
mean everything was so intense and involved
always with tension. My way to experience
emotion was to tighten it up as much as possible,
and not even wittingly. Just 'naturally'. Allen
Ginsberg makes a remark that when I get to

town nobody sleeps till I'm gone. I can't let anybody sleep because I don't want to miss anything. I want it all, and so I tend at times, understandably, to exhaust my friends - keep pushing, pushing, pushing. Not like social pushing to make a big noise, but you know, I don't want to miss it. I love it. I so love the intensity of people that I can't let anything stop until it's literally exhaustion.

INTERVIEWER. I've heard a lot of stories about your fighting in those earlier days.

CREELEY. That's when the confusions of how to be with people became so heightened I would just spill. It had to do with drinking, which I did a lot of in those days. And pot. We were smlking pot pretty continuously by about... let's see...I first had use of marijuana in India, where I was in the American Field Service. We were in a barracks at one point - about forty men, all ages. I think almost everyone in that barracks was turned on almost all day long. We were in Central India. There was literally nothing to do. It was an incredibly awkward climate for us. I mean it was very hot and so we'd sit there sweating - drinking was impossible - and getting very damned sick. I had a friend from Southern California who suggested one day that there was an alternative. He said, 'Try this.' There was nothing mystical. It was very, like, 'Here, have an aspirin.' So the barracks switched and everything became very delightful. The food was instantly palatable and life became much more interesting. So much so

that I remember returning from England on
the Queen Elizabeth and this friend and I
continued smoking a lot of pot on ship. In fact,
we used to go into the toilet. A lot of people
depended on this toilet, and he and I would
get in there and turn on, then sort of sit around.
Outside there'd be this great mass of people
standing and waiting, banging to get in there.
They thought we were homosexuals - a con-
sideration aided by the fact that one night, I
remember, I staggered back into the room
where there were these tiers of bunks, and
trying to get into my bunk I climbed into the
wrong one. We used to get up on the boat deck
too, which was restricted. That North
Atlantic - it was absolutely silent and isolated,
seeing that whole sea in a beautiful full moon.
Just beautiful.

INTERVIEWER. You were talking about fighting.

CREELEY. Well see, with drinking I had the
sense I was drinking in the frustration of
social ineptness. Even to this day if I drink
- I mean up to a point it's extremely pleasant
and relieving and relaxing for me - there
comes a point where my whole feeling turns into
irritation, frustration, and that's when I fight.
I mean, I don't think I ever fought anyone except in that condition - fighting just out of
sheer frustration and a feeling of absolute
incompetence and inability. Also people seemed
very belligerent during the forties and fifties.
We used to get into these ridiculous fights.

INTERVIEWER. I heard you had a fight with

Jackson Pollock once.

CREELEY. Yes, a great meeting. Because he obviously was having the same problem I was, intensively, with a vengeance. I'd been in the Cedar Bar talking with Franz Kline and another friend of Kline's and Fielding Dawson probably was there. We were sitting over at a corner booth, and they were talking and drinking in a kind of relaxed manner. But I, again, you know, very characteristic of me, I was all keyed up with the conversation and I'd start to run to get the beer, or whatever we were drinking and it wasn't coming fast enough. I'd go up to the bar, have a quick drink and return to the table and pick up the drink that by then had come and I was getting awfully lushed and excited and listening and I was up at the bar getting another drink, when the door swings open and in comes this very, you know, very <u>solid</u> man, this very particular man, again, with this intensity. He comes up to the bar, and almost immediately he made some gesture that bugged me. Something like putting his glass on the bar close to mine, that kind of business where he was pushing me just by <u>being there</u>. So I was trying to re-assert my place. The next thing we knew we were swinging at each other. And I remember this guy John, one of the owners, just put his hand on the bar and vaulted, literally, right over the bar, right between us, and he said, like 'Okay, you guys', and he started pushing at both of us, whereupon, without even thinking, we both zeroed in on him and he said, like, 'Come on now, cut it out.' Then he said, 'Do you two

guys know each other?' And so then he introduced us, and - God! It was Jackson Pollock!
So I was showing him pictures of my children
and he was saying, 'I'm their godfather.'
Instantly affable, you know. We were instantly
very friendly. And he was very good to me.
In those days, I remember, in the Cedar Bar,
I had a big wooden-handled clasp knife, that in
moments of frustration and rage - I mean I
never stuck anybody with it, but it was, like
I'd get that knife out, you know, and I don't
think I tried to scare people with it, but I
loved that knife. You could carve things with
it, make things and so on. And so, I'd apparent
been flourishing it in the bar at some point, and
I remember he took it away from me, John did,
and he kept it and said you're not going to have
this knife for two weeks. And then he finally
said, 'Look you can't come in here any more',
and I said, like, 'What am I gonna do? Where
am I gonna go?' So he would finally let me in
if I drank ginger ale only. Because I used to
stand out front and look in the window. Then
he would let me come in and sit, as long as I
was a good boy and drank only ginger ale. And
finally he let me have the knife back, because
that knife was very - well, I've still got one
like it.

INTERVIEWER. When you first took LSD did you
    have any problem?

CREELEY. I had a momentary one, when I
    remember at one point I did enter the dualism
    which is 'yes-no', that binary factor. I felt it
    was going to be absolutely awful. I had just

said something such as 'this is the case' and I
suddenly had an intensive experience of 'this is
the case - this is not the case - this is the
case...' It was like seeing a vast checker-
board - that kind of alternating situation. Then
I just, by grace of something, stepped out of
it. Just stepped out. In the second experience
with it, last summer, blessedly that never
occurred. All through that second LSD
experience I had Donovan's There is a Mountain.
I had a pleasant younger friend and we'd taken
it about two in the morning. We had a fire
burning, and we were in a place in New England.
The day broke clear and fresh and dewy and
there was all this moisture in the trees and
the grass - these spider webs of moisture, and
it was just idyllic. The whole tone of the house
changed. The children had obviously neither
concern nor interest nor knowledge that we
were on LSD, but somehow the feeling went
through the whole house, so that the girls
walked down to a store, maybe a mile away
and bought us a chocolate cake. They also
spent about an hour and a half that morning
making a necklace of pine cones which they
gave Bobbie, my wife. The cats and our dog
were, you know, almost ravenous for us. The
cats were crawling all over us. It wasn't just
our hallucinating and thinking they were; they
were with us every moment - intensively,
rubbing up against us and purring. Then the
fire in the fireplace, that light, beautiful
light; then seeing the dawn come up back of us
as the room began to transform into the day...
So that The Finger is directly, you know, that
information. I remember the business of this

79

primordial experience of woman, in the guise
of my wife; but equally her image floating between the moments of birth - as girl-child to
the most crone-like, the most haggish. Just
crazily - all the guises of woman. All that
Robert Graves, for example, in rather didactic
fashion tries to say is the case. I mean, he's
right, certainly he's right. But it's not a
hierarchy. It's an absolute manifestation
throughout all realms of existence in this
woman figure, and yet woman is woman. She's
unequivocally woman. It was absolutely delightful. I thus 'jiggled a world before her made of
my mind' and I thought, that's the delight.

INTERVIEWER. What do you think is the effect
of hallucinatory drugs on the creative process?

CREELEY. Terrific! That's at least what I'd like
to say. Things had been so uptight, almost for
a year - writing, really our marriage as well,
just a stale sense of effort and also confusions
of feeling older. I think a lot, and at times I
can box myself in with all the rationale of army
logistics. It can get to be a hopeless log jam.
So anyhow the LSD just wiped that out - and
fears and tentativenesses and senses of getting
lost or of being endlessly separated from the
world, all that just went. I can't claim perhaps
so simply that writing was thereby opened but I
do know the past year has felt a very active one
in consequence. The thing is, it's information
- extraordinary and deeply relieving information.
Just as if one were to hear that the war was
over, that some imminent peril and/or bitter
waste of time had stopped. Of course, there's
no need to be told this over and over; that is, I

don't myself feel much need to take the drug every day. It's a vision of a life, all life - and obviously that's a lot to be given by anything or anyone, and so one's not done with it, so to speak, in a day.

INTERVIEWER. When did your interest in painting start?

CREELEY. Well, through Pound's agency I'd come to know René Laubiès, who translated some of Pound's Cantos into French. The first published translation of them into French. And Laubiès was an active and interesting painter. In fact, I saw the first Jackson Pollock I ever really saw in Paris at his gallery, Paul Fachetti's gallery. Up to then my relationships had been primarily with other writers. But I liked Laubiès extremely. It wasn't really the painting as something done that interested me. It was the painter, or the activity of painting I was really intrigued by. About that time I began to look at things. And then, because I was an American living in Europe, having left the New Hampshire farm, I was particularly intrigued by the Americanism of certain painters, like Pollock, obviously, and other friends, like Ashley Bryan, and particularly John Altoon, who becomes very, very important to me because his energies were made so incredibly manifest in his work - images of my own reality so to speak. And then Guston was extremely good to me. I mean, he was very good to me in the sense that he was generous with his interest and time. I was fascinated by the condition of life these guys had. Not simply that they were drinking

all the time, but that they were loners and
peculiarly American, specifically American
in their ways of experiencing activity, with
energy a process - like Pollock's 'When I am
in my painting'. Duncan in his notes on
Maximus makes very clear the relation to
painting that he'd felt in San Francisco with
the group there - Clyfford Still and Diebenkorn
and the whole roster of painters he had as
friends. In writing, everything was still
argued with traditional or inherited attitudes
and forms. And then in the middle 50's, the
painters, without any question, became very
decisive for me personally. And not only for
me. I was thinking about this when I saw John
Ashbery the other day. At one point Ashbery
gave his own sense of the New York School.
He said, 'Well, first of all, the one thing that
we were all in agreement with was that there
should be no programme, and that the poem,
as we imagined it, should be the possibility of
everything we have as experience. There
should be no limit of a programmatic order.'
And then he went on to qualify why painters
were interesting to them. Simply that the
articulation - the range of possibility - in
painting was more viable to their sense of
things. And I thought, 'That's literally what I
would say.' That's precisely the imagination
of the activity I had. All of us are now roughly
in our early 40's, and what's striking is that
each one of us used precisely the same grid of
initial experience and proposal. John was
obviously coming to it by way of the French
Surrealists, where he found, not only playful-
ness, but a very active admission of the world

as it's felt and confronted. It came from other places, too. I was finding it in jazz, for example. And that's why Charlie Parker and Miles Davis and Thelonius Monk and those people were extraordinarily interesting to me. Simply that they seemed to have only the nature of the activity as limit. Possibly they couldn't change water into stone. But then again, maybe they could. That's what was intriguing.

INTERVIEWER. Well, when did you start writing about painters?

CREELEY. I wrote a note about Laubies for the first issue of the Black Mountain Review, which I think is the first note of that order I wrote. Then through the association with Black Mountain, I became very intrigued by Guston and by the visual, what's seen in the world and how all that can be a complex. I'd been so involved with the economy of words, the experience of sound and rhythm, that suddenly it was like having things open again. I wasn't in any sense knowledgeable as to whether this scene had some continuity historically. Nor could I use the vocabulary of the usual art critic. But I could, in Olson's sense, give testament, bear witness to this, to extend an invitation to come. You can see the relevance. We were making things. Not only of our own imagination, which was after all finally the point, but we were making things in the materials particular to our own experience of things, just as John Chamberlain was experiencing the materials in his world, namely

those car parts, and seeing how the imagination
might articulate that experience. I was trying
to make do with the vocabulary in terms of
experience in my world. Neither one of us had
history. I remember Duncan, a lovely moment
when we first met - he and Jess and Harry
Jacoby had come to Mallorca. I was in a
rather dense and difficult time in my marriage.
Ann was away for some reason - down in the
city shopping. We lived in a little house outside of the city. You got there by a trolley
and the four of us were going back into the city
to find them a pension where they could stay.
We were standing in this trolley with all the
people banging around us. I remember Robert
- we were all standing holding straps and he
looked - turned to me at one point and says,
'You're not interested in history, are you?'
I kept saying, 'Well, I ought to be. And I
want to be. But I guess I'm not. You know,
I'd like to be but, no, that's probably true.'
That history, as a form of experience, is truly
not something I've been able to be articulate
with, nor finally engaged by. Art may be, as
Williams might say, the fact of something, but
I did not have that alternative experience of
accepting it as part of a historical progression
in time.

INTERVIEWER. Would you describe something
of the Black Mountain poets - Olson, Duncan,
and the others - and something of those days?

CREELEY. I was first in touch with Olson by way
of Vincent Ferrini. That is, Vincent was a
friend of Cid Corman, and it really is Cid's

magazine Origin, started in Boston in the
early 50's, that makes the centre for all the
subsequent 'Black Mountain school'. I didn't
meet Olson until I went to teach at Black
Mountain in 1954 - which job saved my life in
many ways, and certainly changed it altogether.
Living in Mallorca, despite the ease and
beauty of the place, I'd begun to feel I was
literally good for nothing - so Olson's offer of
a job, and equally his giving me the magazine
to edit, changed that subject completely.

By the time I got to the college, things were
pretty tight. There can't have been more than
twenty or twenty-five students, and every day
it seemed was a kind of last ditch stand. I
remember at one point there was the possibility of some wealthy man in some place like
Charleston sending his mentally deficient son
to us for the benefits of a college education in
exchange for a donation - and after much soul
searching, we agreed. He was to give us word
of his own agreement by having a plane fly
over the college, god knows why - but anyhow
we spent at least three days, all of us,
wandering around the place with eyes to the
sky. I do remember the damn plane never
showed up.

There was another fund raising business that
consisted of Stefan Wolpe, with me as
secretary, writing letters to people like the
Guggenheims and Doris Duke - which Stefan
would begin with, 'I bet you got a lot of money
lying around you don't know what to do with',
and I'd then try to turn it into socially

appropriate English. But nothing ever came
of that either - except for one of the
Guggenheims, who'd apparently just inherited
another bag of gold, sending Stefan a cheque
for ten dollars with a note saying when her
affairs were more in order, she'd try to do
better. De Kooning one time made a lovely
remark about it all, to wit, 'The only trouble
with Black Mountain is, if you go there, they
want to give it to you.'

But for me it was all a revelation, and the
people were terrific. For example, it was
there I met Ed Dorn, Mike Rumaker, Dan Rice
and many, many others. Jonathan Williams
I'd met earlier in Mallorca, and Fee Dawson
was then in the army in Stuttgart - but again
the point is, the intensity and particularity of
the people comprising, like they say, the
Black Mountain scene, was absolute delight.
I suppose the only problem, was, in fact, how
did one find an alternative - which obviously
had to come.

INTERVIEWER. What are the common character-
istics of the Black Mountain group?

CREELEY. I'd almost say - the loner quality each
seems to have. There really isn't a common
idiom, so to speak, as in the New York group,
for example. I think there was a common
feeling that verse was something given one to
write, and that the form it might then take was
intimate with that fact. That's what I at least
meant by 'Form is never more than an extension
of content.'

INTERVIEWER. When did you meet Ginsberg?

CREELEY. In 1956 - after leaving Black Mountain, it must have been in early January or so, then stopping in Albuquerque with friends to pull myself together, then going on to San Francisco where Ed Dorn and his family were. I was trying to get out of my own habits. My marriage had finally ended altogether - and I was sick of what I knew, so to speak. So anyhow I decided to go west. I got to Ed's place about four in the afternoon, and he and Helene drove me around a little. I remember we got very drunk or I at least did - and Rexroth had invited me over for dinner. I can remember vomiting all over the sidewalk, just before I went in, something like an hour or so late. Then later that same night, after Ed had taken off for a job he had as a baggage clerk at Greyhound, suddenly Allen appeared. He was working at the same place only on an earlier shift. It's so characteristic of Allen to be there like that, that is, to come so directly to what interests him. And I was god knows flattered - we talked most of the night about Olson and the scene at Black Mountain. And he told me what was happening in San Francisco. Later, I remember walking around the city with him and Phil Whalen, with Allen inevitably carrying the big black binder notebook, reading us Howl every time we sat down or stopped for something to eat. It was really a beautiful time - everything was so open, just poised on its own energies.

INTERVIEWER. You speak of corresponding with

Williams and Pound. Did you correspond with your contemporaries? What sort of letters?

CREELEY. Insistently. I think at one point Olson and I were writing each other on the average of once every other day. Mayan Letters would give you some sense of it. The fact I was then so far away from everyone meant I depended on letters for a very necessary kind of conversation. Later, living in France, I had Denise Levertov and her husband, Mitch Goodman, to talk to - but more often than not there was really no one immediately available who shared the concerns I was having. Too, I very much needed a practical 'feedback' and letters served that fact. For example, in the early 50's Paul Blackburn and I wrote each other constantly, and he'd give me a very close reading of the poems I'd send him - not just about what he thought they meant, but a literal line to line, word to word, sense of how he took the verse to be moving. So letters were very important to me, and I remember at one point, in Mallorca, calculating I was spending a full eight hours a day writing them. I think it was Williams who said once in a letter that they served as a kind of rehearsal of what it was we were to do.

INTERVIEWER. You have said that poetry is 'the basic act of speech, of utterance'. Are you implying that self-expression is the poet's motivation, or is there more to be said about his desire to communicate, his interest in possible readers?

CREELEY. I don't think that 'possible readers' are really the context in which poetry is written. For myself it's never been the case. If one plays to the gallery in that way, I think it's extraordinarily distracting. The whole performance of writing then becomes some sort of odd entertainment of persons one never meets and probably would be embarrassed to meet in any case. So I'm only interested in what I can articulate with the things given me as confrontation. I can't worry about what it costs me. I don't think any man writing can worry about what the act of writing costs him, even though at times he is very aware of it.

INTERVIEWER. Communication per se, then, isn't a primary motive for the poet?

CREELEY. It is for some; for others, it isn't. It depends on what is meant by communication, of course. I would be very much cheered to realize that someone had felt what I had been feeling in writing - I would be very much reassured that someone had felt with me in that writing. Yet this can't be the context of my own writing. Later I may have horrible doubts indeed as to whether it will ever be read by other persons, but it can never enter importantly into my writing. So I cannot say that communication in the sense of telling someone is what I'm engaged with. In writing I'm telling something to myself, curiously, that I didn't have the knowledge of previously. One time, again some years ago, Franz Kline was being questioned - not with hostility but with some intensity, by another friend - and finally he

said, 'Well, look, if I paint what you know,
then that will simply bore you, the repetition
from me to you. If I paint what I know, it
will be boring to myself. Therefore I paint
what I don't know.' Well, I believe that. I
write what I don't know. Communication is a
word one would have to spend much time
defining. For example, can you make a blind
man see? That has always been a question in
my own mind. And if it is true that you cannot
tell someone something he has no experience
of, then the act of reading is that one is
reading with someone. I feel when people
read my poems most sympathetically, they are
reading with me. So communication is mutual
feeling with someone, not a didactic process
of information.

INTERVIEWER. A side issue here, perhaps.
Does an artist's 'sincerity' have any influence
on the quality of his work? Can a poet write
good poems about a subject if he has no feeling
about it?

CREELEY. I don't see how. If one respects
Pound's measure of 'Only emotion endures',
and 'Nothing counts save the quality of the
emotion', then having no feelings about something seems to prohibit the possibility of that
kind of quality entering. At the same time,
there are many ways of feeling about things;
it may be that - as in the case of poems by
Ted Berrigan - one is made to feel by the fact
that there is no attachment of subjective feeling
to the words. It's a very subtle question. I
remember one time Irving Layton wrote a very

moving poem, Elegy for Fred Smith. Later
Gael Turnbull, very impressed by the poem,
said to him, 'You must feel very badly that
your friend has died, because your poem
concerning this fact is very, very moving.'
And Irving then explained that there was no
man named Smith; he simply wanted to write
this kind of poem. But you see, he wanted the
feeling too; he wanted to gain the way one might
feel in confronting such a possibility. There
wasn't, as it happened, a real fact that pro-
voked this poem, but there was certainly a
feeling involved. And it was certainly a
'subject' that Irving had 'feeling' about. Of
course, this issue of sincerity in itself can be
a kind of refuge of fools. I am sure that
Senator Goldwater was sincere in certain ways,
but that shouldn't protect him from a hostile
judgment. The zealot is often sincere. But I
mean sincerity in the sense that goes back to
Pound, that ideogram he notes: man standing
by his word. That kind of sincerity has always
been important to me - to what I'm doing.

INTERVIEWER. Undoubtedly there are pitfalls,
  too. Edgar Guest was probably as sincere as
  anyone writing today. Why wasn't Guest a
  Williams?

CREELEY. Again, you see, we have a simple
  answer. If we do believe that 'Nothing counts
  save the quality of the emotion,' then we have
  a clear measure for qualifying Guest - the
  emotion in Guest is of very poor quality. It's
  so generally articulated and so blurred with
  assumptional sentiment that it's a kind of mess.

It's too general. So that would be the difference between him, I would feel, and someone like Williams who has the virtue of a much more complex and intimate and modulated quality of feeling - and is much more articulate in the area of that feeling, and not only gives evidence of it, but allows its evidence to be felt by the reader.

INTERVIEWER. This matter of the readers being allowed to feel their way through the poem, the active re-creation of experience. I'm not alone, I think, in feeling excluded from some modern poetry. I was reading the other day a poem by Gary Snyder, How to Make Stew in the Pinacate Desert: 'Now put in the strips of bacon. / In another pan have all the vegetables cleaned up and/ peeled and sliced. / Cut the beef chank meat up small...' If technique is the rationale for Snyder's poem, have we gone too far with the present emphasis on technique?

CREELEY. The context of the poem is very relevant; perhaps I know too much about it. For example, it is addressed to two friends. What Gary's doing here is literally giving them a recipe for stew, and his way of speaking is evident. A tone or mode or kind of speech is occurring. Yes, you can literally take this poem as a recipe for how to make stew, but in this way of saying something there's also an emotional context, a kind of feeling. That, to my mind, is the significant part of this poem. It's the kind of address and the kind of feeling that is engendered by it; and it's the way the words go, literally, that is to me the most intimate aspect of this poem as poem. Now, what can we call it? Technique? Sure, there's technique in that the poem is articulated and held, in the way the words are placed in lines. There's a speed offered in the way the line is going there. But I don't think that he has gone too far, any more than I felt that the actual record of drilling that occurs in Williams' Paterson was going too far. It seemed to be very prosaic, but it gave an extraordinarily vivid sense of how far one did have to dig down to find what was intimate and vital to one's own needs. Just as the water was only to be found after having gone through all those levels, the very character of that report gave a real sense of what it is like to try to find something in an environment that is so covered, so much under the accumulation of refuse, and waste, and tedium, and misuse. So that I would rather not talk in that way of 'technique' as something extensible or separate. And I would have respect for this particular poem of Gary's. Again I fall back on Pound's 'Only emotion endures.' This particular emotion is of an address to friends meant as a warmth which all three shall share, therefore anyone. In that possibility I find the most interest.

INTERVIEWER. Is the remarkable amount of obscenity in contemporary poetry the result of the letdown of barriers - or is it a reflection of the day's mood and temper?

CREELEY. One time Duncan was at a poetry workshop in Arizona, just after Naked Lunch

had been published, and, as he said, the
people were still writing poems about the moon
and the rather indomitable onrush of the spring.
That is, no one really rushed to say 'fuck'
just because it seemed now possible to do so in
print. But then because one did want to be able
to involve a total fact of persons, not just
discreet edges thereof, it was a great relief I
think to be able to do so. No doubt it's me,
but I do think sexual mores have become more
relaxed in the last few years - and obscenity,
or better, the words we so call obscene, have
a very real energy. So one wants use of them
as there seems occasion. I really dig, for
example, Peter Orlovsky's journals that Ed
Sanders has published sections of - not just
for what they tell me of Peter but for what they
make known to me as literal details of sexual
event.

INTERVIEWER. How long does the writing of a
poem take for you?

CREELEY. For me, it's literally the time it
takes to type or otherwise write it - because I
do work in this fashion of simply sitting down
and writing, usually without any process of
revision. So that if it goes - or, rather, comes
- in an opening way, it continues until it closes,
and that's usually when I stop. It's awfully
hard for me to give a sense of actual time
because as I said earlier, I'm not sure of time
in writing. Sometimes it seems a moment and
yet it could have been half an hour or a whole
afternoon. And usually poems come in clusters
of three at a time or perhaps six or seven.

More than one at a time. I'll come into the room and sit and begin working simply because I feel like it. I'll start writing and fooling around, like they say, and something will start to cohere; I'll begin following it as it occurs. It may lead to its own conclusion, complete its own entity. Then, very possibly because of the stimulus of that, something further will begin to come. That seems to be the way I do it. Of course, I have no idea how much time it takes to write a poem in the sense of how much time it takes to accumulate the possibilities of which the poem is the articulation.

INTERVIEWER. Your surroundings during the time both of accumulating and writing - how significant are they?

CREELEY. Allen Ginsberg, for example, can write poems anywhere - trains, planes, in any public place. He isn't the least self-conscious. In fact, he seems to be stimulated by people around him. For myself, I need a very kind of secure quiet. I usually have some music playing, just because it gives me something, a kind of drone that I like, as relaxation. I remember reading that Hart Crane wrote at times to the sound of records because he liked the stimulus and this pushed him to a kind of openness that he could use. In any case, the necessary environment is that which secures the artist in the way that lets him be in the world in a most fruitful manner.

INTERVIEWER. What is your concept of the creative process per se? Would you agree with

Williams' description of it: theoretic know-
how plus 'the imaginative quota, the unbridled
mad-sound basis?'

CREELEY. Yes. One can learn a lot both by
reading and by what you've accumulated by
writing yourself. But then it's up to these
occasions that come without much announce-
ment and declare themselves quite apart from
one's intentions. All the understanding of
process possible doesn't ever guarantee their
occurrence. And one curiously never does
know just when or why or how or in what guise
they will be present.

INTERVIEWER. No one can learn to write poetry,
then? This total involvement of the poet -
experiences, knowledge, technique, emotions
- one is a poet perhaps by virtue of what he is,
not by what he knows?

CREELEY. He's a poet in the sense that he's given
the possibility of poetry by what seems to be a
very mysterious process indeed. Naturally,
all that he knows from his own writing and that
of other writers helps to gain him articulation.
It's rather like driving. A man who can't
drive at all is obviously embarrassed to go
down a road. The most 'articulate' driver
would be one who can follow the road with precisely the right response to each condition
before him. The contexts are in some way
equivalent.

INTERVIEWER. Do you have the sense of
continually progressing - is there a sense in

each successive poem of a new adventure?

CREELEY. A 'new adventure' possibly - that is, like Melville's sense, 'Be true to the dreams of thy youth', which Olson told me Melville had on the wall over his work table. I don't want to be un-romantic about it. But I have never felt I was going anywhere, in writing - not like, 'Every day, in every way, I am getting better and better'. What I've really loved is the fact that at times I can take place in this activity, just be there with whatever comes of that fact. I live in this house, or with my wife, in just the same way. It's not 'getting somewhere' that is the point of it all.

INTERVIEWER. You have spoken of a poem being created almost 'in a fit', or in a seizure. Does it ever bother you to think that these attacks may not come? It seems such an American phenomenon to believe that the force of inspiration disappears in time.

CREELEY. It bothers me very damn much - but I've never found a cure for it. I don't know another writer who hasn't faced the same dilemma. But I don't know what one can do about it except hold on. I did realize finally that at times I was perversely enjoying my discontent, that is, I was all but wallowing in the inertia I felt I was stuck with. That's quickly a bore. But it's still true, of my own experience, that no amount of wanting to do something can actually make writing possible.

INTERVIEWER. Well, do you consciously choose

your subjects?

CREELEY. Never that I've been aware of. I may make too much emphasis upon that, but I can't remember ever consciously setting out to write a poem literally about something. Well, I can think of an exception. That would be a sequence of poems done to complement Robert Indiana's Numbers - but after roughly a year of frustrated attempts to write these poems, the first five came to me, quite literally, between the hours of five and seven in the morning - a time I've never found possible for writing nor for much of anything else.

For myself, writing has always been the way of finding what I was feeling about, what so engaged me as 'subject' and particularly to find the articulation of emotions in the actual writing. So, I don't choose my subjects with any consciousness whatsoever. I think once things have begun - that is, once there are three or four lines, then there begins to be a continuity of possibility engendered which I probably do follow. And I can recognize, say, looking back at what I have written that some concerns have been persistent; the terms of marriage, relations of men and women, senses of isolation, senses of place in the intimate measure. But I have never to my own knowledge begun with any sense of 'subject'. I fall back on that point of Olson's - I think it's Letter 15 in the Maximus poems where it goes: 'He sd, "You go all around the subject" and I sd, "I didn't know it was a subject."'' You see,

I don't know that poetry has 'subjects' except as some sort of categorical reference for listing in library catalogues. Poetry has themes, that is, persistent contents which occur in poetry willy-nilly with or without the recognition of the writer. These themes are such as Olson once spoke of, war, love between man and woman, friendship, and the care of the earth. But I don't feel that these 'subjects' are really the primary indication of the poem's merit or utility in the society in which it is present.

INTERVIEWER. You don't, then, have any 'point' to make, to use a common term of reference?

CREELEY. The point I wish to make is that I am writing. Writing is my primary articulation. So when I write, that's what I'm at work with - an articulation of what confronts me, which I can't really realize or anticipate prior to the writing. I think I said in the introduction to The Gold Diggers, well over ten years ago, that if you say one thing it always will lead to more than you had thought to say. This has always been my experience.

INTERVIEWER. To look a little more closely at the 'themes', then, in your work. Many seem to deal with love, hate - in short, human relationships. Is this human interaction the dominant interest from an artistic point of view?

CREELEY. Well, I've always been embarrassed

for a so-called larger view. I've been given
to write about that which has the most intimate
presence for me, and I've always felt very,
very edgy those few times when I have tried to
gain a larger view. I've never felt right. I
am given as a man to work with what is most
intimate to me - these senses of relationship
among people. I think, for myself at least,
the world is most evident and most intense in
those relationships. Therefore they are the
materials of which my work is made.

INTERVIEWER. Then, in general, are you
writing about what is personally most important
to you?

CREELEY. Yes. People are the most important
things in the world for me. I don't at all mean
that in a humanistic sense. It's just that they
are the most insistent and most demanding and
most complex presences offered to me.

INTERVIEWER. In some ways, this kind of
subject is different from that of many of
Williams' poems, which you admittedly admire.
Is there a contradiction here?

CREELEY. Again, remember what Williams does
say, 'The poet thinks with his poem.' When he
has a poem such as the Red Wheelbarrow,
which occurs in that sequence Spring and All, a
mixture of poetry and prose in its original
version, that poem, and that whole sequence,
is a way of perceiving - not decided upon but
met, almost in full course, by 'divine accident'
as Stendhal would say. Williams says that

particular sequence moves among the recognitions given him from his perceptions. That's what I am interested in, in those poems - not the literal material evident in the red wheelbarrow, but in how the perception occurs, how he thinks in the context of that relationship. Not simply why he says this, but how he says it, how he gives it credence, how he gives it recognition. We are both doing something quite akin: we're thinking, we're gaining an articulation for ourselves in the activity of the poem. As he says, 'In our family we stammer until, half mad, we come to speech.' Or he says, 'the words made solely of air.' This context for poetry is one very intimate and immediately recognizable to myself. So I don't think that you can say, 'Well, this man talks about green bottles and this man talks about his wife; therefore, they are not interested in the same things.' It's the way these things are perceived in the poem and how they are articulated that is significant; and in that respect I would feel a great debt to Williams and would feel that I had learned much from him indeed.

INTERVIEWER. Since two recent books are prose, The Island and the re-issue of The Gold Diggers, could we talk for a while about the differences between poetry and prose?

CREELEY. Well, prose seems to offer more variety in ways of approaching experience. It's more leisurely. One can experiment while en route, so to speak. But still, for me, poetry gives a more immediate, a more concentrated articulation - a finer way of speaking. I don't prefer either. I don't say poetry is more useful for me in this sense, and prose in that sense, and therefore I write a story when I want this effect, and a poem when I want that effect. They come and go. When something has been on my mind for a long, long time and I've been in some sense conscious of it, then very often it will be prose that gives me the chance of articulating what is dogging me with such emotional insistence. I think, for example, of a park in England where I was sitting with a friend; and I was very new to our surroundings. I felt not alien but freshly arrived. We were sitting in this quiet park on a Sunday afternoon, a small sort of intimate family park with walks, not hidden exactly, but arranged so that people moved along through corridors of trees and plants, so that one had a constantly changing vista of persons as they came and went. And there was a kind of old statue, not particularly distinct or admirable but sort of interesting, as if a kind of old person had suddenly been immobilized or concretized. But in any case, that moment, sitting on that bench, talking in this rather random fashion and watching the people and seeing children all ages, impressed itself on my mind. I don't know what I'm going to do with it - or rather, I don't know what it's going to do with me. But that kind of insistence - it's one of the most intense things which I seem to have gained in England. I don't know what it means. I don't understand it. I don't know why - of all the kinds of experience that I had there - that moment suddenly is awfully intense. But at some moment that's probably something that's coming to be written. I feel it now, that it's coming, that I shall work with it. And when I do work with it, I would feel it will probably be with prose because it has such a complexity in it that I'll want to move with it tentatively. Prose may give me a way of feeling my way through such a thing. Poetry is more often a kind of absolute seizure - a demand that doesn't offer variations of this kind.

INTERVIEWER. So prose is very much in your future, as well as poetry?

CREELEY. I must say that as soon as I plan to do more prose, I do absolutely nothing. I had planned to do another novel, because I really enjoyed The Island, having learned in a sense some of the technical possibilities of such a form - that is, having written it - I gained some insight into what technically was possible in a long prose piece. I wanted not to lose it, so I very quickly committed myself to do another novel, which was unwise of me. I even gave the novel a title, and had what I thought was a good occasion (two years I spent in Guatemala had given me a crazily chaotic impression of so many things and persons and acts - such a wild variability of people in such a very curiously primal place - that I thought, this is an ideal thing to work with in prose). But as soon as I planned to do it, I all but stopped. I don't know how I am going to get past that. One day I'll simply sit down and start writing. Until that day comes, talking about it is a little absurd because I simply don't work in that fashion. By planning to do the novel, and by talking about it with my publisher, accepting a small advance and giving it this title and all, I seem - well, one moment last spring, for example, I really got almost hysterical and I called the publisher and said, 'Look, I want to pay you back that money. I'm sick to death of the whole programme.' No, again, you see, Pound is so right. That quote he has from Rémy de Gourmont, 'Freely to write what one chooses is the sole pleasure of a writer.' That is so true. So that as soon as it becomes programmed in any way, in the sense that it isn't momently recognized, it's a very, very problematic context in which to try anything.

INTERVIEWER. Were your short stories written usually in one movement? Like the poems?

CREELEY. Right. Again that's why I say that the kind of economy that Pollock was speaking of was very real to me...when he said, 'When I am in my painting...' I remember one time in the 50's a conversation Guston was having with my first wife. She'd challenged him: 'If you're painting this way, abstract-expressionism or whatever you call it, how do you know when it's done?' She really was suggesting that he was in some way a phony, and that everything he was involved in was in some way phony. He took the question seriously, and gave her a very careful and generous statement of his own experience of painting. His resolution was that you know when it's done when you are both looking at and involved with what's happening, and you can't see any place where further

activity is permitted. I mean, where everything has happened. And I knew that was
precisely how I felt about writing, that when I
couldn't say anything more, that was the end.
You continued writing and/or speaking until
no further possibility of continuing was there.
And I thought this was what these particular
men as Kline, or as Guston, or as De Kooning
- not De Kooning so much because his formal
procedure was rather different - but Pollock,
absolutely - that they were not so much
'experimenting', but that they were delighted
and moved and engaged by an activity -
permitted an experience of something - and
that they were with it as long as it was possible
to be. And at some point it ended. I mean it
stopped, and they were thus pushed out, or
made to stop too, and that was it.

INTERVIEWER. There exists at the moment a
large group of young poets writing what have
been called by some 'Creeley poems'. Short,
terse, poignant - at their best. You know, of
course, you have tremendous influence on the
generation to come. Do you think this influence
is good?

CREELEY. I haven't the least idea. That's up to
them to demonstrate. At a poetry conference,
Robert Duncan - hearing many poems dedicated
to himself - said, 'My God, do I really sound
like that?' There's a kind of horror in seeing
what's taken from one's own acts as the
significant aspect of them, played back. This
kind of active feedback provides a very interesting
disarrangement and what people make of my

work in this way has sometimes delighted me
and sometimes left me very disgruntled. But
I don't think it's up to me to decide whether
it's good or bad. It will demonstrate its own
virtues or failures.

INTERVIEWER. Where can these young writers
move in this imitative writing?

CREELEY. Again, I haven't the least sense of
where they can go in their poetry. That is very
much their own business - as it was mine and
remains mine. We return to that sense of
Olson's that each of us has his own 'kin and
concentration'. So that for me to propose
large rules for all poets would be absurd. I
feel simply that all those engaged as poets can
take what they will from what I may have
discovered or from what those before me have
discovered or what men after me will discover.
Obviously, there's no end to it, but I believe it
should all be handed over and that it can or
cannot be used as each person learns for himself.

INTERVIEWER. What is the pattern? Will these
young writers stay imitative?

CREELEY. No, they won't. Imitation is a way
of gaining articulation. It is the way one learns,
by having the intimate possibility of some
master like Williams or Pound. Writing poems
in those modes was a great instruction to me
when I began to 'feel' what Williams was doing
as well as 'understand' it. This imitative
phase is a natural thing in artists. I feel it

106

should be encouraged. It is one way to learn,
and it's the way I would respect, coming as I do
from a rural background where learning how to
plough is both watching someone else do it and
then taking the handle of the plough and seeing
if you can imitate, literally, his way of doing
it, therefore gaining the use of it for yourself.
But what you then plough - and whether you
plough or not - is your own business. And
there are, fortunately, many ways to do it.

(Linda Wagner, Lewis MacAdams, Jr.
Paris Review Xl, Autumn 1968)

1. Why do you continue to write? What purpose
does your work serve? Do you feel yourself
part of a rear-guard action in the service of a
declining tradition? Has your sense of vocation
altered significantly in recent years?

'Because it 's there to be written, ' as William
Carlos Williams said. I don't really know if
there is more reason that that, in relation to some
sense of purpose or intent. There are clearly
things I've wanted to do in writing - specific
forms I've wanted to try, as a novel, for example,
or diverse ways in which an active seriality
might be manifest. But the primary occasion in
writing is a situation I've never been able to
design, even when I've much wanted to.

Thinking then of why one continues - that's equally
inexplicable, except that it is, literally, an active
possibility for me, in my life. It keeps happening
and the way the world then enters, or how I'm also
then known to myself, is a deeply fascinating
circumstance. Charles Olson makes a lovely
point, that 'we do what we know before we know
what we do, ' and that really is the delight in
writing, that much happens one has no conscious

information of until it is there, in the words.
I'm not thinking here of some sort of do-it-yourself
psychoanalysis - that's of no interest to me - but
a deeper fact of revelation I feel very actual in
writing, a realization, reification, of what is.

The tradition to which I relate comes, as Robert
Duncan would say, 'from a well deeper than time.'
It's not yesterday's news one is concerned with.
However one thinks to qualify it, the fact of being
a poet teaches one that it is not an ego-centered
occupation but a trust one had really no thought to
undertake. But there it was. Suddenly. One
morning. With the birds. I'm trying to say that
poetry comes from a tradition far more complex
and rooted in the human condition than any one
'time' can define. Better to consider Konrad
Lorenz's sense of tradition as he speaks to it in
his book On Aggression - the intuitive economy of
human experience, biological and environmental
in this case.

As to my sense of vocation - for a long time I was
very tentative about saying in any forthright
manner that I was a poet. It seemed extraordinarily presumptuous. But again, it's not a
vocation one can earn, however one respects the
responsibility of this literal 'calling'. In any case,
being a poet is something I can acknowledge more
clearly in my own nature at this point. It seems
a consistently present reality, although I respect
a qualification a friend, Max Finstein, once made:
that one is a poet in the act of writing, not otherwise.

However, I realize the nature of this question has

really to do with a sense of literary tradition, and
vocation as some form of professional occupation,
etc. I've always been an amateur insofar as I
loved what I did. Olson said that Melville had
over his work table the statement: 'Be true to the
dreams of thy youth'. I respect that commitment
deeply. If anything, I feel a deep blessing and
good fortune in what my 'vocation' has given me
as a sense of my life. Saying that - it seems
suddenly a little convenient, in a way, but I do
feel blessed by life, no matter that at times it is
difficult and painful.

2. Do you believe that art and politics should be
   kept apart? Has this belief changed or grown
   more complicated during the past decade?
   What influence has the politicization of life
   during this period had on your work?

Having come of age in the forties (I started
college the summer of 1943), 'politicization' was,
it then seemed, so much a part of that time I
don't know that it seems more so now. Perhaps
it's some sort of weird sandwich one is experiencing
with the blandness of the fifties intervening, the
bread being the forties and sixties. But having
been in some ways active in the Henry Wallace
party, also having been taught politics by the YCL
while still in college - it doesn't seem to me that
life is now more political. It certainly isn't quite
as didactic, let's say, as was the membership of
the PAC - or any friends then involved with post-
war Marxism. I don't think there is quite the
same insistence on the 'right' and 'wrong' ways

that there was then.

Possibly political agency is regaining an active contest. But really the advanced younger people of this moment are, if anything, post-political, just that the available political agencies seem to them so bankrupt. The militant part of the black community might be the one active revolutionary group still intent on political possibilities. I know that many of the young showed an active commitment to Eugene McCarthy's leadership in the circumstances of the 1968 election, but I question, even with reluctance, that that had initially to do with political occasion or possibility. More, I think, they wanted renewal of a kind of presence, in public life, possessed of a demonstrable integrity, even one apart from the usual conditions of political activity. They wanted someone to be literally there - and this was, curiously, not the case either with Kennedy or Nixon. Both were finally part of a system the young have every reason to distrust, as, God knows, the elders might equally.

Obviously the disaster of the national commitment to the war in Vietnam is the largest 'political' counter of the past few years and it served to energize political agencies in every sense. But again, I'm very intrigued by the hippie culture, so to speak, and its decisively apolitical character. It's as though a very deep shift in the conception of human relations and use of the environment were taking place - and indeed I very much believe that it is. We've come to that time when, as Williams said, we must either change our 'wishes' or perish. I don't feel that present insistence on ecological problems is simply a new game. We have literally to change our minds. In this respect, drugs in the culture have really two, among other, clear possibilities: (1) either to reveal a oneness in all manifestations of life-form of whatever order and thus change the mind by that revelation (certainly the most useful information to be gained from taking LSD); or (2) to kill anxiety, to lull intuitive perception of inherent peril, to simply get out of the 'world' one is actually in - and in this respect the elders are as committed to this use of chemical agency as any of the young.

In any case, I don't see that art and politics, or that order of present experience involved with the post-political, should all be kept separate. I don't see how they can be. One can't, perhaps, entirely respect an art committed to propagandizing or to a use of life not clearly initiated in its own activity. But when men and women are outraged by political malfeasance, it's hardly likely that their art will not make that quite clear.

As far as my own work is concerned - I've not been able to write directly to a purpose of political involvement. It's not given me in my own nature to be able to do so, but I hope that I've made clear where I stood nonetheless. I hate the out-rage of human beings that present political acts now effect. One must protest them - they are literally against life itself.

3. What are the main creative opportunities and problems that attract and beset you in your work? Which movements, tendencies, writers,

if any, do you find yourself identifying with or
supporting? Which ones do you oppose?

It's difficult to qualify just what 'creative
opportunities and problems' are primary. Just
that something does come to be said, is an
opportunity of very great magnitude. Too, poetry
as I've had experience of it is not, finally, at the
service of other conditions or orders of information,
however much it may serve them once it exists.
Olson says that art is the only true twin life has
- in that either is not to a 'purpose' apart from the
fact of themselves. They don't <u>refer</u>, so to speak.
There's no <u>excuse</u>.

The 'problems' occur when one loses his way in
such possibility, muffs or misuses the nature of
what's given. It is, again as Olson says, something as actual as wood, or fish, that one has to
do with. It's not in the mind in some sense that
one can now exercise a discretion upon it -
thinking about it in some privileged way. On the
contrary, there is a feeling that adamantly does
insist one is being told something and had better
get it right the first time, else there won't be
another chance. One is told <u>once</u>. For this
reason I find it hard ever to <u>revise</u> - 're-see' -
just because the initial seeing has to be responded
to with all the ability possible because I'm not
given another chance. It's very like seeing someone you do respond to in the instant and having
thus the choice of going home and thinking about it,
or making that response a manifest act. I agree
with Robert Duncan that choice is recognition -
not a debate between alternatives. So if one doesn't

know 'what to do', given such circumstances, clearly there's nothing really to do.

Otherwise I'm not much concerned with either creative opportunities or problems. I love a particular poem by Kenneth Koch, beginning something like, 'Thank you for giving me this battleship to wash...' Thank you for giving me creative opportunities, i.e., I wonder what a woman would say to that.

'Movements, tendencies, writers...' There is a company, a kind of leaderless Robin Hood's band, which I dearly love. I'm sure there is even a horn to summon us all. There is no company dearer, more phenomenal, closer to my heart. A few weeks ago I happened to spend the night at Allen Ginsberg's farm and coming down to the kitchen in the morning, met with Allen's charming remark, 'All the poets are up!' Which very truly we were, Lawrence Ferlinghetti, Gregory Corso, Allen and myself - while five others also there slept on.

Whether learned by intuition or by act, one comes to respect and to love that company of writers for whom poetry is, in Bob Rose's phrase, 'active transformation', not a purpose, not discretion, not even craftsmanship - but revelation, initial and eternal, whatever that last word can mean to one whose life is finite. Consequently I both identify with and support - and hope I might be permitted the company of - any man or woman whose experience of writing transcends some sense of its value as money in the bank, or edifying addition to one's identity, etc. None of the so-called Black Mountain writers wrote in a literally similar manner. That is, Olson's modes of statement are certainly not mine, nor are they Duncan's, nor Denise Levertov's - and so on. What was, then, the basis for our company? I think, simply the insistent feeling we were given something to write, that it wasn't something we could 'think' to write, that it was an obedience we were undertaking to an actual possibility of revelation. Which to say one might own would be absurd.

What I find abhorrent is any assumption that one has gained the use of writing as a private con- venience, to me the ugliest of all attitudes.

4. Has writing entered a 'post-modern' era, in which the relevance of the great modern writers (Joyce, Eliot, Mann, Faulkner, et al.) has declined? If so, what seem to be the literary principles of the post-modern age? If not, what principles of modernism are still dominant and valuable?

Supposing 'modern' to define the primary conscious- ness of a decisive shift in the conception of reality, which becomes increasingly clear toward the end of the nineteenth century, then one may feel that that consciousness is now a general condition in human experience. The world cannot be 'known' entirely. Certainly it cannot, in the way men are given to live in it and to know it, be 'perfected'. In all disciplines of human attention and act, the possibilities inherent in the previous conception of a Newtonian universe - with its containment and thus the possibility of being known - have been yielded. We do not know the world in that way, nor will we. Reality is continuous, not separable, and cannot be objectified. We cannot stand aside to see it.

Writing, and all of the arts as well, have entered the altered consciousness of men's situation in the world. One might speak, possibly, of 'the modern' as the first impact of that realization in the arts: Eliot expressing both regret for pre- viously possible order and recognition of the new experience of how the world happens - simply what takes place. Yeats, in a late note on modern poetry, understandably with frustration, speaks of modern poets as asking us to 'accept a worth- less present'. If one thinks then quickly of Samuel Beckett's use of that 'present', where to be lasts but an instant where every instant/ spills in the void the ignorance of having been', a measure of the change involved is apparent.

Much that the modern writers got said seems to me still of great relevance. Both Williams and Pound - or Lawrence, Stein, H.D., and many others also - point up the dilemma of what may be called individual sensibility in an environment insistently generalizing all circumstances of apprehension and decision. That problem hardly seems solved. However, what is at first feared as a loss of coherence - felt most in the loss of history's authority - starts to become less that as other situations of experience occur. High and low art begin to melt as historical valuations blur. All being now, all that is there has possibility.

The ego's authority tends to relax and conceptions
involved with proposals of 'good, better, best'
also lose ground. Most interesting to me is the
insistent presence of what has been called the
chance factor in the activity of all the arts of the
past several years. Whether in 'happenings' or
in the music of younger composers like Cornelius
Cardew, one sees that a discipline, so to speak,
is being gained to discover a formal possibility in
a highly variable context of activity. It may well
be that 'beauty' is simply being returned to 'the
eye of the beholder', but what the eye expects to
see is nonetheless much altered.

Still it does seem that terms such as 'modern'
and 'post-modern' are habits of art history. One
tends to use all that he can get hold of and I don't
know that one 'time' is thus distinct from another,
in the actual practice. Here is where one seems
to be.

5. Has there been a general collapse of literary
   standards in recent years? Are you conscious
   of a conflict between your past standards and
   your present ones?

I remember an incident, like they say, involving
a critic I much respect, Warren Tallman, and an
Englishman, in a radio discussion of Jack Kerouac's
Big Sur for CBC. Warren was plugging for
Kerouac's genius in being able to make so articulate
and substantial all the data of the senses. What
impressed Warren was the fact that when some
thing or activity was spoken of, one's experience

of it was extraordinarily vivid. The Englishman,
however, felt that some canon of literary form
had been broken. When Warren pushed him to
qualify just what 'standard' he was referring to,
the man hedged, unable actually to state it - then
said, 'Well, we know enough to know these
standards exist, even if we don't know what they
are.'

Kind of a wistfully moving point, actually. But I'm
extraordinarily wary of any 'standard' not the
direct result of an active experience in the practice
of the art involved. Or as Olson puts it, 'telling
me what in the instant I knew better of,' and this
is not by any means an egocentric response to
'rules' imposed by taste and opinion, that have
nothing to do with the nature of the language and
all the possibilities therein. Pound quotes Remy
de Gourmont, 'Freely to write what he chooses is
the sole pleasure of a writer' - and I agree with
that utterly. 'Standards' are only interesting in
relation to the possibilities they recognize. In
the forties I felt them arbitrarily restrictive and
dominated by the practice of criticism apart from
the practice of poetry itself.

So far from feeling there has been a collapse of
literary standards, I feel there has been a
reconstitution of them in the practice of writing
itself. Think of the victories actually won:
relaxation of censorship in the use of specific
words, admission of serial order as a complex
and diversely organized phenomenon, a riddance
to all senses of 'poetic subject', poems bien fait
to some dull mould, and so on. The list is happily
a long one, In short, I think that such standards

as poetry involves and they exist unequivocally,
are again the issue of the practice - not a viciously
parasitic addendum put on the practice of poetry
by men in no wise committed to it.

My past standards continue to be my present
ones. I permit myself possibly more freedom
now - not by a relaxation, but in the broader
range of perception I am able to respond to in
writing, in the degrees of emotional condition I
find I can speak. Man standing by his word -
Pound's translation of the Chinese ideogram for
sincerity - stays as my own measure, but I have
begun to apprehend too the complexity of that
situation. It's not a simple honesty, etc.

6. Has literary criticism and journalism kept
   pace with, and faith with, the best fiction,
   poetry, and drama produced in the sixties?

A lovely novelist we know, world-famous no less,
writes on a Christmas card just received: 'For
Christ's sake keep up the good work and don't be
sidetracked by Christmas or the goddam reviewers
who are ugly people...' As far as I'm concerned
and speaking particularly of the situation of poetry,
there is no correspondence of any interest to me
between the activities in contemporary criticism
and that poetry I am myself most engaged with.
Even if one considers a particular critic of
intelligence, Richard Howard, who is also a writer
of poems, the score is still lousy. In his book,
Alone With America, Essays on the Art of Poetry
in the United States Since 1950, there are gaps I

so deeply question that the book itself becomes a
fine instance of mandarin writing - i.e., an
'entertainment' of 'sensibility'. And he is, in my
own estimation, perhaps the best. Where
'journalism' may be in any of this, I simply don't
know. Reviews are either so tardy or so absent
one can hardly consider them as 'keeping pace'.
A fellow wrote recently to tell me he'd been asked
by The Nation to review my collection Words for
one of their coming issues. The book was
published in 1967. Pieces, a subsequent collection
of poems, was published last August, and possibly
that might be reviewed in the far, far distant
future. But really, one hardly depends on it.

The point is, if one meets with an exceptional
critical intelligence - e.g., Kenneth Burke, D.H.
Lawrence, Edward Dahlberg, Ezra Pound - then
that's the point, not 'literary criticism'. Joshua
Whatmough says, in a book called Language, that
literary criticism is just an exchange of opinion
and has no authority in relation to the activities
it criticizes. That cheers me up. When younger,
I was not 'criticized' at all. Now older, it seems
I rarely do things right, or five years ago I did
them right, not now. As for literary criticism
'keeping faith' - I didn't know it had faith to keep.
If one is thinking of men active in the arts making
notes, etc., then the whole question obviously
changes.

(New American Review, December 21, 1969)

SIGNATURE is a new series of shorter works,
distinguished by the highly personal and
imaginative approach of the author to his subject.
It comprises works of poetry and prose, fiction
and non-fiction, and includes English, American,
and translated texts.

POETRY FROM CALDER & BOYARS

THE COLLECTED POEMS OF JAMES AGEE -
Ed. Robert Fitzgerald
The hitherto unpublished collected poems of this
revered American literary figure. £2.25*

ZONE - Guillaume Apollinaire
A bilingual edition of Apollinaire's famous poem,
translated by Samuel Beckett. £1.75*

FLOWERS OF EVIL - Charles Baudelaire
A bilingual edition of the collected verse of the
great French poet of sin and retribution. £2.50*

AN ANTHOLOGY OF MEXICAN POETRY - Tr.
Samuel Beckett, Ed. Octavio Paz
A selection from the work of 35 Mexican poets,
writing between 1521 and 1910, translated by
Samuel Beckett. £2.10*, £1.05+

POEMS IN ENGLISH - Samuel Beckett
This volume of pre-war poetry shows Beckett to
be a major poet as well as a great prose-stylist.
£1.05*, 60p+

THE FINGER - Robert Creeley
Poems that are beautifully precise and subtle in
phrase and imagery. £1.75*, 95p+

POEMS 1950-1965 - Robert Creeley
'His tiny but intricate compositions read like charms
or incantations...Creeley is a real poet and an
exceedingly serious artist.' (The Guardian).
£1.75*, 90p+

THE CHARM - Robert Creeley
Poems memorable for the simplicity of their
content and style. £1.50*, 75p+

PRISON POEMS - Yuli Daniel
A unique, bilingual record of Daniel's poetic
achievement. 'An important and necessary book.'
(Sunday Times). £1.50*, 75p+

A BLACK MANIFESTO IN JAZZ, POETRY &
PROSE - Ted Joans
Works to be read aloud, to be listened to with the
unrestrained ear reserved for the best of jazz.
£1.50*, 60p+

A BLACK POW-WOW OF JAZZ POEMS - Ted Joans
An exciting collection of the best poems of this
highly talented black artist. £1.75*

DARKER ENDS - Robert Nye
Poems by turns tender, beautiful and intense in
their vision. £1.05*, 50p+

COLLECTED POEMS - Raymond Radiguet
A bilingual edition of the complete verse of this
brilliant poet. £2.00*

NEW RUSSIAN POETS - Ed. George Reavey
A collection of poems by distinguished Russian
writers, including Pasternak and Yevtushenko.
£2.50*

ECLIPSE - Alan Riddell
A compelling collection of concrete poetry. £2.50*

CONTEMPORARY SCOTTISH VERSE -
Ed. Alexander Scott & Norman MacCaig
Two hundred and forty poems by modern Scottish
poets, ranging from Hugh Mac Diarmid (b. 1892)
to Alan Bold (b. 1943). £1.75*, 75p+

POETRY OF YEVGENY YEVTUSHENKO -
Ed. George Reavey
Poetry that reflects the aspirations of the young
in Russia. Bilingual edition. £2.50*, £1.25+

LITERARY CRITICISM

COLLECTED WORKS, VOL. 1 - Antonin Artaud
Contains the important correspondence with
Jacques Rivière, together with many of his most
significant miscellaneous writings.
£2.50*, £1.00+

COLLECTED WORKS, VOL. 2 - Antonin Artaud
Contains the early formulations of his theories
on theatre in general and the genesis of the 'theatre
of cruelty. ' £2.75*, £1.30+

COLLECTED WORKS, VOL. 3 - Antonin Artaud
Contains the film scenarios that are quite extraordinary precursors of modern underground
movies. £2.95*

COLLECTED WORKS, VOL. 4 - Antonin Artaud
Contains The Theatre And Its Double, the famous
group of essays embodying the essence of Artaud's
revolutionary theories, and The Cenci, an
historical drama based loosely on Shelley's poem.
£3.00*

COLLECTED WORKS, VOL. 5 - Antonin Artaud
Contains the famous Heliogabalus and the correspondence with André Breton.   £3.00*

GRAHAM GREENE - John Atkins
A profound and enjoyably readable study of the
works of the greatest living English writer.
                                               £2.50*

ALDOUS HUXLEY - John Atkins
An indispensable companion volume to the works
of Huxley, tracing his philosophical and creative
development.   £2.25*

GEORGE ORWELL - John Atkins
A biographical study of the author of 1984 and
Animal Farm and how his life affected his creative
work.   £3.25*

SEX IN LITERATURE: VOL. 1 - John Atkins
The first volume of a comprehensive study of the
erotic impulse in literature analyses, among
other works, the amatory sonnets of the Restoration
and twentieth-century erotology.   £3.15*

SEX IN LITERATURE: VOL. 2 - John Atkins
Analyses the sexual impulse in the major Greek
and Roman writers.   £3.50*

THE MODERN ENGLISH SOCIAL NOVEL - John
Atkins
A fascinating study of the English social novel
from 1920 to 1970 through the work of L.P. Hartley,
Evelyn Waugh and others.   £3.00*

LITERATURE AND EVIL - Georges Bataille
Fascinating essays which trace the influence of
evil in writers such as the Bronte sisters, Blake
and Sade.   £3.00*

THE MARQUIS DE SADE - Simone de Beauvoir
A brilliant study of one of the most controversial
figures in history.   £1.25*, 90p+

PROUST & 3 DIALOGUES WITH DUTHUIT -
Samuel Beckett
A superb critical study of Proust, the first great
European novelist, by the outstanding writer of
the present day.   £1.25*, 60p+

BERTOLT BRECHT - Frederic Ewen
A brilliant biography which has been hailed as 'the
finest critical study of Brecht to date'. (Los
Angeles Times)   £4.20*

NEW DIRECTIONS IN LITERATURE - John Fletcher
Deals with the advent of the 'nouveau roman' in
post-war France. 'A very worthwhile book...
Fletcher is good at conveying why it is exciting to
read these authors'. (The Listener)
                                       £2.00*, 90p+

RAYMOND ROUSSEL - Rayner Heppenstall
A sympathetic and perceptive study of one of the
foremost surrealist authors.   £1.25*, 60p+

NOTES & COUNTERNOTES - Eugene Ionesco
A fascinating volume of theatrical essays by one
of the most profoundly influential playwrights of
the last 20 years.   £1.25*, 90p+

PRESENT PAST: PAST PRESENT - Eugene
Ionesco
Thoughts and memoirs movingly linking the author's
plays with his miserable early life.   £2.25*

REVELATION IN SHAKESPEARE - R.W.S. Mendl
An authoritative survey of the supernatural,
spiritual and religious elements in Shakespeare's
works.   75p*

THE WORLD OF TRUMAN CAPOTE - William L.
Nance
The first major analysis of Capote's writings and
artistic life links his personal with his creative
existence.   £2.50*

SNAPSHOTS & TOWARDS A NEW NOVEL - Alain
Robbe-Grillet
Contains the author's collected critical writings,
with the author's own declaration of what modern
literature is and a clear and highly original view
of the world.   £1.50*, 90p+

TROPISMS & THE AGE OF SUSPICION - Nathalie
Sarraute
Remarkable critical essays by one of the foremost
creators of the 'nouveau roman'.   £1.25*, 75p+

* Cloth
+ Paperback